When you find yourself STUCK…

RISE
ABOVE THE SITUATION

RECOGNIZE
Recognize that you
re stuck.

IDENTIFY
Identify what **exactly** is getting in the
way of making better progress

STRATEGIZE
Create some "clever systems" to deal with the
problem

EVALUATE
Evaluate how well your strategies are working and
change them as needed

Name_____

Tel. No._____

Email _____

School _____

Grade____ Homeroom _____

THE HOMEWORK ORGANIZER can help you the most if you use it correctly, consistently, and completely. Select the features you want to use (start small — with one/some that will be most helpful to you), and check them off below.

[For a detailed list of contents, see the Index on the last page]

This assignment notebook contains:

 ❑ A **FINDER SYSTEM** to help make sure you remember—before you leave school—the materials you'll need to do each assignment

 ❑ A **LONG TERM ASSIGNMENT GUIDE** to help you finish on time—and without last minute panic—the assignments that are due a few days, a week, or a month away

 ❑ A **FIVE DAY FORECAST TIME PLANNER** to help you manage your time so you can fit in your homework and still have time for "extracurricular" activities

 ❑ **INSTRUCTION ON HOW TO WRITE A CHECKLIST** to help you stay organized and focused on your more important "To Do's" and not get distracted by less important things

 ❑ A **TEACHER TRACKER** so that you can find your teachers when you need them

 ❑ A **STUDY LINKS DIRECTORY** of classmates to call when you're stuck

 ❑ **GRADE SAVER RECORD KEEPERS** so you know where you stand with your grade in any subject at any given moment, and you aren't taken by surprise at report card time

 ❑ **SUPERSTRUCTURE OPTIONS** to improve your chances of succeeding even more

 ❑ **STRATEGY STRAIGHT TALK** tips to help you get and stay organized!

❑ **HOMEWORK TIPS** for getting your homework started, finished, and turned in on time

INSTRUCTIONS

Assignments for the week of **OCTOBER 2 – 6** ①

WEDNESDAY

SUBJECT ✓	🖐 FINDER	ASSIGNMENT ②	DUE ③
MATH			
SCIENCE			
HISTORY/ SOC. STUDIES ✓ ⑤	④	READ P. 48-72, ANSWER Qs #1-8	THUR.
ENGLISH/ LANG. ARTS			
SPANISH		RESEARCH PICASSO ONLINE	NEXT MON.
LONG TERM ASSIGNMENT	STRATEGIC TIP	NEXT	

OTHER THINGS TO REMEMBER 🖐 GYM CLOTHES   X _____

---

① Write the week's **DATES** at the top of the page.

② Locate the subject for the assignment. Fill in the **ASSIGNMENT** with **specific details** on the page, the action you need to take and the item numbers to complete. **If there is no assignment, write "None."**

③ Then write in the **day or date the assignment is DUE.**

④ In the 🖐**FINDER,** circle the **materials you'll need** to do the assignment. (📓 = spiral notebook, 📂 = 3-ring binder, 📄 = worksheets, 📕 = text book) Check the **Finder before you leave school** to remind you what to take home.

Add **ANYTHING ELSE** you need to remember for the next day in the "Other Things To Remember 🖐" space.

⑤ **When you have finished the assignment,** mark the subject's ☑ **CHECK OFF** box.

(On the daily assignment page...)

Go to the **FIVE DAY FORECAST. MAKE A PLAN** for doing your homework:

• First,

SCHEDULE IN

and/or block out any activities, work hours, appointments and social or family commitments from the time schedule.

• Then, **WRITE IN**

your assignment where you know you'll have time to do it (and so that it's done before the due date!).

TIME TRACKER OPTION

🕐 **ESTIMATE** in your head **how long** you think the assignment will take to finish.

🕐 **WRITE** your estimate in the **subject box** (where the digital number prompt barely appears)

🕐 Consider this estimate when you **make your PLAN** in the Five Day Forecast.

🕐 To get even more precise, **CHECK** your estimate against the **actual time** it took you!

SUPERSTRUCTURE OPTIONS

In some circumstances more structure can make the difference between a successful and an unsuccessful student. If you and your parent(s) or teacher(s) think this would make the difference for you, decide which options below "fit" you and check the ones you'll use. Modify the agreement as needed.

SUBJECT		ASSIGNMENT	DUE
			1	**2**
SPANISH		RESEARCH PICASSO ONLINE	*JLR*	NEXT MON. *JLR*
LONG TERM ASSIGNMENT		PLANNING STRATEGIC TIP NEXT	
OTHER THINGS TO REMEMBER	GYM CLOTHES	X_____	**3**

1 To make sure I have written the assignments correctly and completely and I have highlighted the correct materials to bring home:

☐ I will have the **TEACHER** sign his/her initials in the assignment box after checking what I wrote.

2 To make sure I remembered to pass in my homework:

☐ I will have my **TEACHER** sign his/her initials in the "due" box when I have passed in my homework.

3 To make sure I remembered to do all the homework that was assigned:

☐ I will have my **PARENT** sign at the "X" to show that he/she has seen my assignment notebook and my finished work to match it. This can also be used as a teacher or parent "comment space."

_____(student) agree to use the options checked above to help myself be a better student.

_____(parent) agree to use the parent option to help my child be a better student.

agree to use the teacher options(s) to help my student be more successful. (Teachers' signatures):

	Options (circle)		Options (circle)
_____	1 2	_____	1 2
_____	1 2	_____	1 2
_____	1 2	_____	1 2

A STRATEGY is... a clever system that helps you do something better, faster, or more easily.

— Gail Epstein Mengel, Ph.D.

HOMEWORK TIPS

Check off each "tip" after you have read it. Then highlight the ones you plan to use.

☐ **COORDINATE** your textbook covers, notebooks, class schedule, and divider tabs (in your 3-ring binder) to match in **color** for each individual subject. **This will help you FIND ALL THE MATERIALS you need for each subject more quickly.**

☐ When you write down the assignment, **remember** to include all the details you need to know to do it: the **P**age, the **A**ction you must take, and the **I**tem **N**umbers (a memory trigger is "**PAIN**"). **This will help you to START WORKING without getting frustrated.**

☐ If you tend to put off doing assignments till the last minute, try this: As soon as you get home, take a step—no matter how small—toward doing the assignment. A small step might be setting up your book on the table to the right page and putting a heading on your paper. Setting **short term objectives** like this helps you feel as if you have crossed the "threshold" to doing your homework. **This SMALL STEP will make it easier to get started doing your assignment.**

☐ Start with a short easy assignment just to get yourself going, but do your hardest homework early in your study routine. Leave simpler work for last. **This will make it easier for you to FINISH ALL YOUR HOMEWORK.**

☐ Make a **TIME SANDWICH**: Estimate how much time each assignment will take to finish. Look at your study periods and after school schedule. Match the assignments to the blocks of time you have and "sandwich" them in. Always check your estimates after you finish to see how accurate you were at estimating and adjust your estimates, if you need to, for the next time. **This will help you ORGANIZE YOUR TIME better.**

☐ If you only have small blocks of time to do your homework, use the **NIBBLE METHOD**: **Smash** your homework assignment into smaller steps or parts. **Nibble away** a part of the assignment at a time. Before you know it, your small nibbles will have finished the whole assignment! **This will help you use the time you have more efficiently.**

☐ Decide where **exactly** you will put your finished homework for each subject. It helps if you choose only ONE central place where you put it—a special "homework folder" or a spring clip attached to your 3-ring binder. **This will help you FIND YOUR HOMEWORK more easily when you need to turn it in.**

☐ As soon as you finish an assignment, put it immediately in the spot you have chosen. When you finish all your homework, be sure to put it into your backpack, and place your backpack by the door you leave in the morning. **This will help you to bring all your homework to school the next day and SAVE YOU TIME searching for your school things last minute.**

☐ Set up rewards for yourself (milk and cookies, a TV show) for doing your homework. Realistically decide how much work you will do before you take a break. **After** you have finished what you planned to do, give yourself the reward. **This will help LINK SOMETHING POSITIVE with finishing your homework and make it a more pleasant task.**

STRATEGY STRAIGHT TALK

A STRATEGY is... a clever system that helps you do something better, faster, or more easily.

Throw out every piece of paper you can!

Don't let paper build up. Always be on the lookout for pieces you can trash. Figure out and write down the criteria or categories for what you think can be *stashed* or *trashed*. These criteria will help you make decisions with less effort. For those papers you know you will definitely need to keep, write "SAVE" at the top the first time you handle them. Enjoy the good feeling that comes from getting rid of excess paper.

Use this strategy for keeping your desk, notebook, or backpack more organized.

Write "NEXT:_____"

...before you leave a multi-stepped task and fill in the blank with the very next step. This helps you recognize immediately where you need to begin, so you don't have to take time "spinning your wheels" trying to remember where you left off!

Use this strategy when you're doing a lab report or when working on a long term assignment.

Start small, start anywhere, JUST START!

Look for anything that "calls out to you" and that you *know* you can start organizing. Once you have crossed the "line" of getting organized, it is much easier to keep going!

Use this strategy when you need to clean your room—what "calls out" may be a basket that needs emptying, some pencils that need to be put back in a container, or some books that need to be reshelved.

START

Group objects and papers into categories...

using "containers," "dividers," or "separators." These should be "hard-edged" (for example, baskets, binder pockets, file folders, pencil holding cans, stacking trays, subject dividers, shelves, etc.—not plastic bags). Collect things-of-a-kind together and label them with a summary name or a graphic. Then designate a place for everything so everything has its own place. This makes it easier for things to be put back in their rightful places with less effortful thinking.

Use this strategy to separate out supplies in your desk—your writing utensils, art/graphic supplies (markers, colored pencils, etc.), paper supplies (graph paper, lined, and blank paper).

Do all of one step, part, place or category at a time...

before you move on to the next one. This helps you feel the gratification and satisfaction more immediately of having finished something.

 EXAMPLES **Use this strategy for cleaning up your bedroom—pick up all the things on your floor (place), or put all the books away (category), or throw out everything that is trash (step).**

et up a checklist of things to do

...before you start an overwhelming job. This helps you stay more focused as you begin a task that can be hard to approach. It also gives you a built-in yardstick to mark off your progress with the task.

EXAMPLES **Use this strategy to get make-up work done after an absence.**

If you tend to forget things,

place them with something you KNOW you will remember to do or take with you, or somehow attach it.

EXAMPLES **Use this strategy if you tend to forget your gym clothes—place them on your sneakers the night before you have your gym class.**

et up an if-in-doubt policy.

If you aren't sure what to do in certain situations, set up a clearcut policy for yourself to follow.

EXAMPLES **Use this strategy if there is any doubt about whether to take a book home for the night or not—The "if-in-doubt" policy is—take it home!**

'se mnemonics (nem on ics)

— memory tricks — to trigger memory of a procedure or routine.

EXAMPLES Try **PAIN**: write the assignment's **P**age, **A**ction to take, and **I**tem **N**umbers to do when recording your assignment.

Make an organizational routine

into a habit so that if it is NOT done, it "feels like **something is missing.**"

It helps to do the steps of the routine in the same order each time. This creates a "chain" memory that triggers you to think of the next step when you finish the step just before it.

EXAMPLES **Use this strategy to get your backpack ready for the next day—put in your homework, books, and your lunch money in the same order each time.**

- ☐ **SMASH THE TASK** into its smaller bits and pieces.

- ☐ **SMASH THE BITS AND PIECES** into even **smaller** bits until they are bite-sized enough to feel do-able. If you can say to yourself, "I can do that," you have succeeded in reducing them into small enough steps.

- ☐ Use **ACTION** words to guide the **exact** action to take (ex., read, find out, finish, write, call, buy, make, figure out, see, decide).

- ☐ Decide which, of all the bits and pieces, are the very 👉 **NEXT STEPS** to take. If the steps need to be done in a certain order, determine which come first and sequence them.

- ☐ Write your list with **CHECKBOXES** so you can check off when you finished each task, or draw a line through each thing on the list as you do it.

- ☐ **TITLE THE CHECKLIST** (Ex., To Do, Project, Lab Report, Cleaning Room).

- ☐ **ATTACH** the checklist to your everyday assignment pages for easy reference (use sticky notes or a paperclip).

Example: Making up work after an absence.

MAKE UP WORK

- ☐ Figure out dates I was absent
- ☐ Look at class schedule for those dates
- ☐ List the classes I had on those dates
- ☐ See my teachers about the assignments I missed
  - ☐ Check Teacher Tracker
  - ☐ Schedule to see each teacher
- ☐ Find out when the make up assignments are due.
- ☐ Write them in my Homework Organizer

SEE HOW GOOD IT FEELS WHEN YOU CROSS THINGS OFF YOUR LIST!

We smashed this step into even smaller steps.

GRADE SAVER I (weighted average)

NAME: _____   SUBJECT: _____   TEACHER: _____

QUESTIONS TO ASK ABOUT THE GRADING POLICY:

1. What measures are included in averaging your grade? 2. How is each of these weighted in averaging your grade? 3. What lowers your grade (ex., late hand-ins)? 4. What can raise your grade (ex., extra credit work)? 5. What is the make-up policy? 6. How is your grade computed? Write the grading policy on the blank side of your COPIED Grade Saver.

TESTS

	Date	Description	Grade
1			
2			
3			
4			
5			
6			
7			
8			
9			
10			
11			
12			
13			
14			
15			
16			

End of Term Average.

QUIZZES

	Date	Description	Grade
1			
2			
3			
4			
5			
6			
7			
8			
9			
10			
11			
12			
13			
14			
15			
16			

End of Term Average.

	Date	Description	Grade
1			
2			
3			
4			
5			
6			
7			
8			
9			
10			
11			
12			
13			
14			
15			
16			

End of Term Average.

AVERAGE

Date	Average

End of Term Average.

STOP Write only on COPIES of this page.

DIRECTIONS:

First: **MAKE COPIES** of this page for each subject and secure **THE COPIES** firmly in your notebook or Homework Organizer. **Next: ON YOUR COPIES**, write in the types of measures included in your grade (tests, quizzes, labs, projects, papers) at the top of each column above. **Tips:** (1) Look for patterns among your lower grades to see where you need to focus more effort. (2) figure out your average often to see "where you stand" with your grade.

GRADE SAVER 2 (point system)

	① Date	② Description	③ Score	④ Max Value	⑤ Sum of ③ ÷ sum of ④	⑥ Calculated Average	⑦ Letter Grade
1							
2							
3							
4							
5							
6							
7							
8							
9							
10							
11							
12							
13							
14							
15							
16							
17							
18							
19							
20							
21							
22							
23							
24							

DIRECTIONS:

① Write the date. ② Write the description of the test or measure, etc. ③ Record your score. ④ Enter how many points this test or measure was worth. ⑤ Find the sum of all your **scores** in column 3 and divide this by the sum of all the **maximum values** in column 4. ⑥ The result of this calculation is your **average.** ⑦ Find the corresponding letter grade that matches this average:

SAMPLE

	① Date	② Description	③ Score	④ Max Value	⑤ Sum of ③ ÷ sum of ④	⑥ Calculated Average	⑦ Letter Grade
1	10/15	Test—continents	85	100	85÷100	85	B
2	10/23	Quiz—Animals of S.A.	7	10	92÷110	84	B
3	11/3	Project—Animal habitats	49	50	141÷160	88	B+
4	11/18	Test—Unit	95	100	236÷260	91	A-
5	11/26	Pop quiz	4	5	240÷265	91	A-
6	12/5	Notebook check	6	10	246÷275	89	B+

Average required for A=____to____ B=____to____ C=____to____ D=____to____

STOP Write only on COPIES of this page.

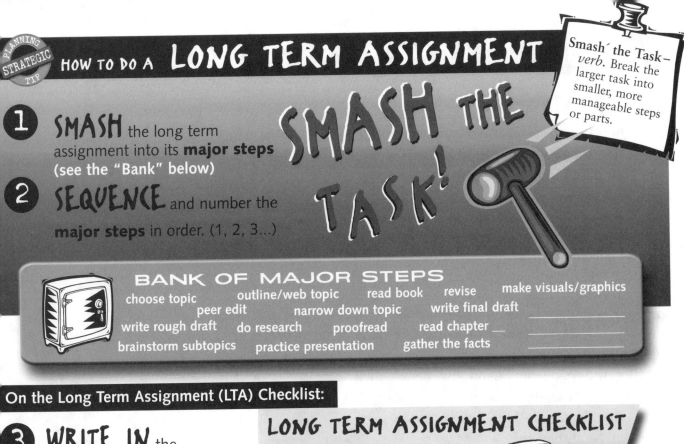

Smash´ the Task– *verb.* Break the larger task into smaller, more manageable steps or parts.

1 **SMASH** the long term assignment into its **major steps** (see the "Bank" below)

2 **SEQUENCE** and number the **major steps** in order. (1, 2, 3...)

SMASH THE TASK!

BANK OF MAJOR STEPS

choose topic   outline/web topic   read book   revise   make visuals/graphics
peer edit   narrow down topic   write final draft
write rough draft   do research   proofread   read chapter __
brainstorm subtopics   practice presentation   gather the facts

---

On the Long Term Assignment (LTA) Checklist:

3 **WRITE IN** the **major steps** in order.

4 **SMASH** the major steps into **everyday actions** you can take daily and write these in **under each major step** on the LTA checklist.

5 **ESTIMATE** the time (in days) needed to complete each **step** and write this on the clipboard graphic.

Estimated Days Needed

6 **ADD UP** the total number of days needed. Check to make sure your total number of days doesn't take you past the due date! Confirm with your instructor that your plan is workable.

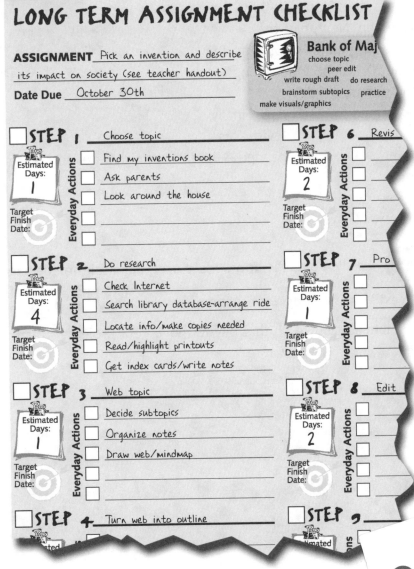

LONG TERM ASSIGNMENT CHECKLIST

Bank of Maj
choose topic
peer edit
write rough draft   do research
brainstorm subtopics   practice
make visuals/graphics

ASSIGNMENT Pick an invention and describe its impact on society (see teacher handout)

Date Due October 30th

☐ **STEP 1** _Choose topic_
Estimated Days: 1
☐ Find my inventions book
☐ Ask parents
☐ Look around the house
☐
☐
Target Finish Date:
Everyday Actions

☐ **STEP 2** _Do research_
Estimated Days: 4
☐ Check Internet
☐ Search library database-arrange ride
☐ Locate info/make copies needed
☐ Read/highlight printouts
☐ Get index cards/write notes
Target Finish Date:
Everyday Actions

☐ **STEP 3** _Web topic_
Estimated Days: 1
☐ Decide subtopics
☐ Organize notes
☐ Draw web/mindmap
☐
☐
Target Finish Date:
Everyday Actions

☐ **STEP 4** _Turn web into outline_

☐ **STEP 6** _Revis_
Estimated Days: 2
Target Finish Date:
Everyday Actions

☐ **STEP 7** _Pro_
Estimated Days: 1
Target Finish Date:
Everyday Actions

☐ **STEP 8** _Edit_
Estimated Days: 2
Target Finish Date:
Everyday Actions

☐ **STEP 9**

7 **ADJUST** your estimated time for each **major step** as necessary. Plan your work so you finish one step before you start the next. Now, **lightly** pencil in your target finish dates on the LTA checklist for each major step.

Target Finish Date:

8 Go to the appropriate **monthly calendar** in the back of your Homework Organizer. Cross out days you have reserved for other comittments.

BEGIN AT THE DUE DATE

and count backwards the total number of days needed. (Add 2 extra days for breathing room.) This is the "Start date" for the first step. Next, plot the remaining **major steps** onto the monthly calendar according to the number of days you estimated for each step. Finally, revise – as

Target Finish Date:

needed – the target finish dates for each step on your LTA checklist.

OCTOBER

Sunday	Monday	Tuesday	Wednesday	Thursday	Friday	Saturday
			1 Start: Choose Topic	2 Start Research	3 ✗	4 ✗
5 Research →	6	7	8 Web Topic	9 Outline	10 ✗	11 ✗
12 ✗	13 Rough Draft →	14	15	16 Start Revise	17 ✗	18 ✗
19 Revise	20 Proof Read	21 Start Edit →	22	23 Start Final Draft	24 ✗	25 ✗
26 Final Draft →	27	28 Do Visuals	29	30 LTA Due	31	

9 Lastly, go to the appropriate **everyday assignment pages**. Over the word "Next" on the Long Term Assignment line, **WRITE THE EVERYDAY ACTIONS** you'll need to take on that day to move your project forward.

10 CHECK your real progress with your written plan often, and readjust your scheduling if you need to.

LONG TERM ASSIGNMENT CHECKLIST

ASSIGNMENT_____

_____

Date Due _____

Bank of Major Steps

choose topic   outline/web topic   read book   revise

peer edit   narrow down topic   write final draft

write rough draft   do research   proofread   read chapter ___

brainstorm subtopics   practice presentation   gather the facts

make visuals/graphics   _____   _____

☐ **STEP 1** _____

Estimated Days:

Target Finish Date:

Everyday Actions

☐ _____
☐ _____
☐ _____
☐ _____
☐ _____

☐ **STEP 2** _____

Estimated Days:

Target Finish Date:

Everyday Actions

☐ _____
☐ _____
☐ _____
☐ _____
☐ _____

☐ **STEP 3** _____

Estimated Days:

Target Finish Date:

Everyday Actions

☐ _____
☐ _____
☐ _____
☐ _____
☐ _____

☐ **STEP 4** _____

Estimated Days:

Target Finish Date:

Everyday Actions

☐ _____
☐ _____
☐ _____
☐ _____
☐ _____

☐ **STEP 5** _____

Estimated Days:

Target Finish Date:

Everyday Actions

☐ _____
☐ _____
☐ _____
☐ _____
☐ _____

☐ **STEP 6** _____

Estimated Days:

Target Finish Date:

Everyday Actions

☐ _____
☐ _____
☐ _____
☐ _____
☐ _____

☐ **STEP 7** _____

Estimated Days:

Target Finish Date:

Everyday Actions

☐ _____
☐ _____
☐ _____
☐ _____
☐ _____

☐ **STEP 8** _____

Estimated Days:

Target Finish Date:

Everyday Actions

☐ _____
☐ _____
☐ _____
☐ _____
☐ _____

☐ **STEP 9** _____

Estimated Days:

Target Finish Date:

Everyday Actions

☐ _____
☐ _____
☐ _____
☐ _____
☐ _____

☐ **STEP 10** _____

Estimated Days:

Target Finish Date:

Everyday Actions

☐ _____
☐ _____
☐ _____
☐ _____
☐ _____

TOTAL NUMBER OF DAYS:

LONG TERM ASSIGNMENT CHECKLIST

ASSIGNMENT_____

_____

Date Due _____

Bank of Major Steps

choose topic   outline/web topic   read book   revise
peer edit   narrow down topic   write final draft
write rough draft   do research   proofread   read chapter ___
brainstorm subtopics   practice presentation   gather the facts
make visuals/graphics   _____   _____

☐ STEP 1 _____

Estimated Days:

Target Finish Date:

Everyday Actions
☐ _____
☐ _____
☐ _____
☐ _____
☐ _____

☐ STEP 2 _____

Estimated Days:

Target Finish Date:

Everyday Actions
☐ _____
☐ _____
☐ _____
☐ _____
☐ _____

☐ STEP 3 _____

Estimated Days:

Target Finish Date:

Everyday Actions
☐ _____
☐ _____
☐ _____
☐ _____
☐ _____

☐ STEP 4 _____

Estimated Days:

Target Finish Date:

Everyday Actions
☐ _____
☐ _____
☐ _____
☐ _____
☐ _____

☐ STEP 5 _____

Estimated Days:

Target Finish Date:

Everyday Actions
☐ _____
☐ _____
☐ _____
☐ _____
☐ _____

☐ STEP 6 _____

Estimated Days:

Target Finish Date:

Everyday Actions
☐ _____
☐ _____
☐ _____
☐ _____
☐ _____

☐ STEP 7 _____

Estimated Days:

Target Finish Date:

Everyday Actions
☐ _____
☐ _____
☐ _____
☐ _____
☐ _____

☐ STEP 8 _____

Estimated Days:

Target Finish Date:

Everyday Actions
☐ _____
☐ _____
☐ _____
☐ _____
☐ _____

☐ STEP 9 _____

Estimated Days:

Target Finish Date:

Everyday Actions
☐ _____
☐ _____
☐ _____
☐ _____
☐ _____

☐ STEP 10 _____

Estimated Days:

Target Finish Date:

Everyday Actions
☐ _____
☐ _____
☐ _____
☐ _____
☐ _____

TOTAL NUMBER OF DAYS:

LONG TERM ASSIGNMENT CHECKLIST

ASSIGNMENT_____

_____

Date Due _____

Bank of Major Steps

outline/web topic   read book   revise

peer edit   narrow down topic   write final draft

write rough draft   do research   proofread   read chapter ___

brainstorm subtopics   practice presentation   gather the facts

make visuals/graphics   _____   _____

☐ STEP 1 _____

Estimated Days:

Target Finish Date:

Everyday Actions
☐ _____
☐ _____
☐ _____
☐ _____
☐ _____

☐ STEP 2 _____

Estimated Days:

Target Finish Date:

Everyday Actions
☐ _____
☐ _____
☐ _____
☐ _____
☐ _____

☐ STEP 3 _____

Estimated Days:

Target Finish Date:

Everyday Actions
☐ _____
☐ _____
☐ _____
☐ _____
☐ _____

☐ STEP 4 _____

Estimated Days:

Target Finish Date:

Everyday Actions
☐ _____
☐ _____
☐ _____
☐ _____
☐ _____

☐ STEP 5 _____

Estimated Days:

Target Finish Date:

Everyday Actions
☐ _____
☐ _____
☐ _____
☐ _____
☐ _____

☐ STEP 6 _____

Estimated Days:

Target Finish Date:

Everyday Actions
☐ _____
☐ _____
☐ _____
☐ _____
☐ _____

☐ STEP 7 _____

Estimated Days:

Target Finish Date:

Everyday Actions
☐ _____
☐ _____
☐ _____
☐ _____
☐ _____

☐ STEP 8 _____

Estimated Days:

Target Finish Date:

Everyday Actions
☐ _____
☐ _____
☐ _____
☐ _____
☐ _____

☐ STEP 9 _____

Estimated Days:

Target Finish Date:

Everyday Actions
☐ _____
☐ _____
☐ _____
☐ _____
☐ _____

☐ STEP 10 _____

Estimated Days:

Target Finish Date:

Everyday Actions
☐ _____
☐ _____
☐ _____
☐ _____
☐ _____

TOTAL NUMBER OF DAYS:

LONG TERM ASSIGNMENT CHECKLIST

ASSIGNMENT_____

_____

Date Due _____

☐ **STEP 1** _____

Estimated Days:

Target Finish Date:

Everyday Actions

☐ _____
☐ _____
☐ _____
☐ _____
☐ _____

☐ **STEP 2** _____

Estimated Days:

Target Finish Date:

Everyday Actions

☐ _____
☐ _____
☐ _____
☐ _____
☐ _____

☐ **STEP 3** _____

Estimated Days:

Target Finish Date:

Everyday Actions

☐ _____
☐ _____
☐ _____
☐ _____
☐ _____

☐ **STEP 4** _____

Estimated Days:

Target Finish Date:

Everyday Actions

☐ _____
☐ _____
☐ _____
☐ _____
☐ _____

☐ **STEP 5** _____

Estimated Days:

Target Finish Date:

Everyday Actions

☐ _____
☐ _____
☐ _____
☐ _____
☐ _____

☐ **STEP 6** _____

Estimated Days:

Target Finish Date:

Everyday Actions

☐ _____
☐ _____
☐ _____
☐ _____
☐ _____

☐ **STEP 7** _____

Estimated Days:

Target Finish Date:

Everyday Actions

☐ _____
☐ _____
☐ _____
☐ _____
☐ _____

☐ **STEP 8** _____

Estimated Days:

Target Finish Date:

Everyday Actions

☐ _____
☐ _____
☐ _____
☐ _____
☐ _____

☐ **STEP 9** _____

Estimated Days:

Target Finish Date:

Everyday Actions

☐ _____
☐ _____
☐ _____
☐ _____
☐ _____

☐ **STEP 10** _____

Estimated Days:

Target Finish Date:

Everyday Actions

☐ _____
☐ _____
☐ _____
☐ _____
☐ _____

TOTAL NUMBER OF DAYS:

"The single best way to deal with a job that is daunting, unpleasant, or – simply – just has to be done, is to

SMASH THE TASK

Break it into its smaller bits and pieces and then tackle them...

one by one."

— Gail Epstein Mengel, Ph.D.

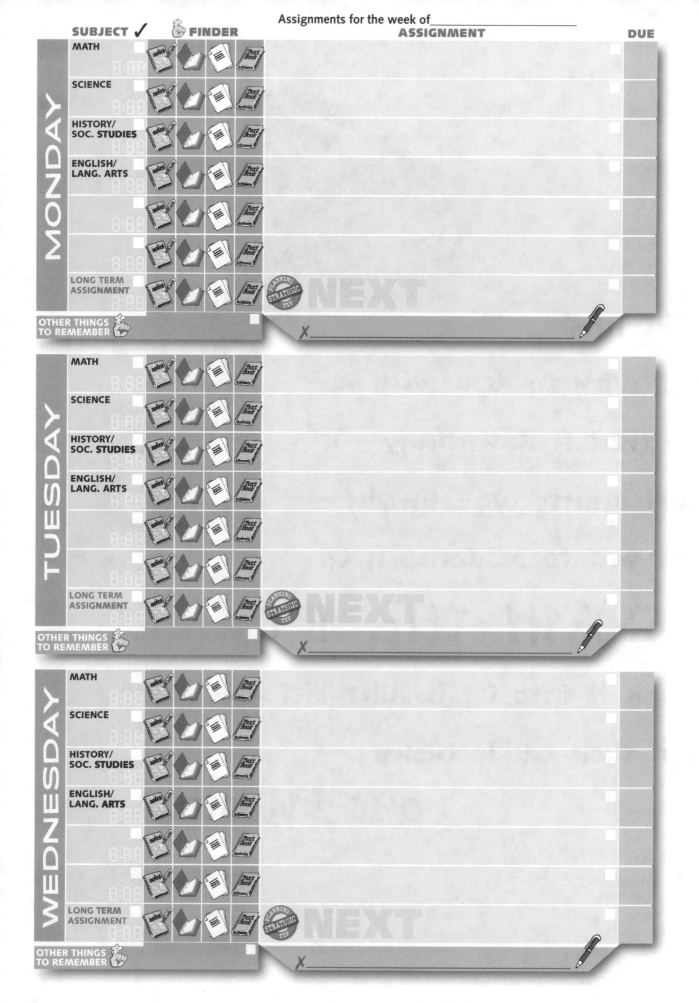

SUBJECT ✓	🐾 FINDER	ASSIGNMENT	DUE
THURSDAY			
MATH	notes 📁 📄 Text Book		
SCIENCE	notes 📁 📄 Text Book		
HISTORY/ SOC. STUDIES	notes 📁 📄 Text Book		
ENGLISH/ LANG. ARTS	notes 📁 📄 Text Book		
	notes 📁 📄 Text Book		
	notes 📁 📄 Text Book		
LONG TERM ASSIGNMENT	notes 📁 📄 Text Book	STRATEGIC TIP NEXT	
OTHER THINGS TO REMEMBER		X _____	

SUBJECT ✓	🐾 FINDER	ASSIGNMENT	DUE
FRIDAY			
MATH	notes 📁 📄 Text Book		
SCIENCE	notes 📁 📄 Text Book		
HISTORY/ SOC. STUDIES	notes 📁 📄 Text Book		
ENGLISH/ LANG. ARTS	notes 📁 📄 Text Book		
	notes 📁 📄 Text Book		
	notes 📁 📄 Text Book		
LONG TERM ASSIGNMENT	notes 📁 📄 Text Book	STRATEGIC TIP NEXT	
OTHER THINGS TO REMEMBER		X _____	

FIVE DAY FORECAST

	MONDAY	TUESDAY	WEDNESDAY	THURSDAY	FRIDAY
BEFORE SCHOOL					
DURING SCHOOL					
AFTER SCHOOL					
EVENING					
BEFORE BED					
Homework	READY TO GO ☐	READY TO GO ☐	READY TO GO ☐	READY TO GO ☐	READY TO GO ☐

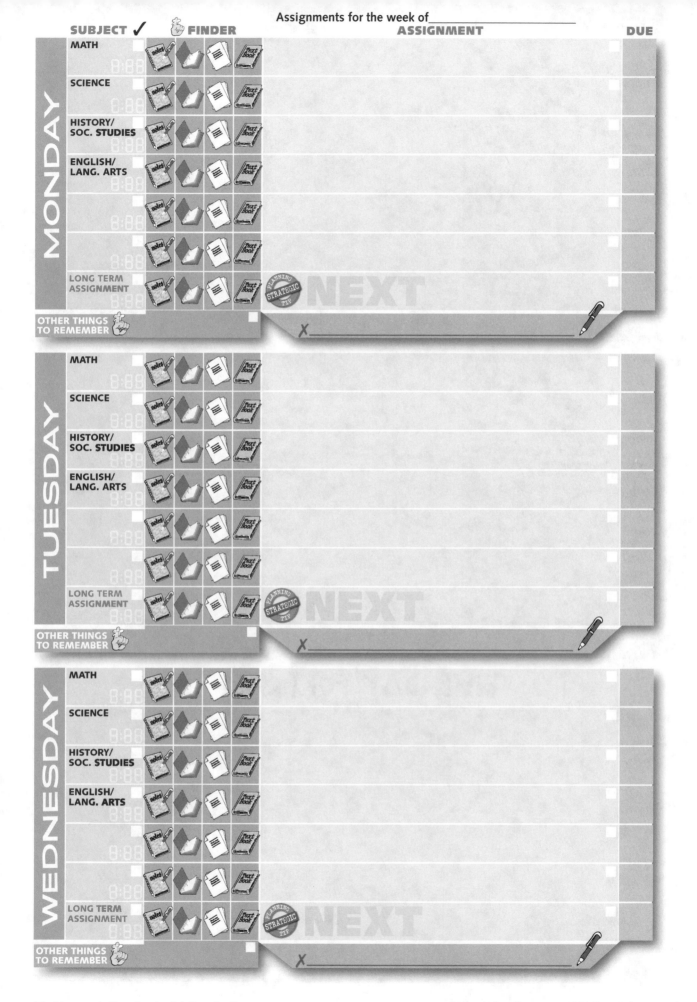

Assignments for the week of_____

SUBJECT ✓	FINDER	ASSIGNMENT	DUE

MONDAY

MATH
SCIENCE
HISTORY/ SOC. STUDIES
ENGLISH/ LANG. ARTS
LONG TERM ASSIGNMENT — NEXT
OTHER THINGS TO REMEMBER
X_____

TUESDAY

MATH
SCIENCE
HISTORY/ SOC. STUDIES
ENGLISH/ LANG. ARTS
LONG TERM ASSIGNMENT — NEXT
OTHER THINGS TO REMEMBER
X_____

WEDNESDAY

MATH
SCIENCE
HISTORY/ SOC. STUDIES
ENGLISH/ LANG. ARTS
LONG TERM ASSIGNMENT — NEXT
OTHER THINGS TO REMEMBER
X_____

SUBJECT ✓   FINDER   ASSIGNMENT   DUE

THURSDAY

MATH	notes	Text Book
SCIENCE	notes	Text Book
HISTORY/ SOC. STUDIES	notes	Text Book
ENGLISH/ LANG. ARTS	notes	Text Book
	notes	Text Book
	notes	Text Book
LONG TERM ASSIGNMENT	notes	Text Book

NEXT

OTHER THINGS TO REMEMBER

X_____

FRIDAY

MATH	notes	Text Book
SCIENCE	notes	Text Book
HISTORY/ SOC. STUDIES	notes	Text Book
ENGLISH/ LANG. ARTS	notes	Text Book
	notes	Text Book
	notes	Text Book
LONG TERM ASSIGNMENT	notes	Text Book

NEXT

OTHER THINGS TO REMEMBER

X_____

FIVE DAY FORECAST

	MONDAY	TUESDAY	WEDNESDAY	THURSDAY	FRIDAY
BEFORE SCHOOL					
DURING SCHOOL					
AFTER SCHOOL					
EVENING					
BEFORE BED					
Homework	READY TO GO	READY TO GO	READY TO GO	READY TO GO	READY TO GO

www.homework-organizer.com • © 2002 Gail Epstein Mengel   The Homework Organizer by Get Organized!

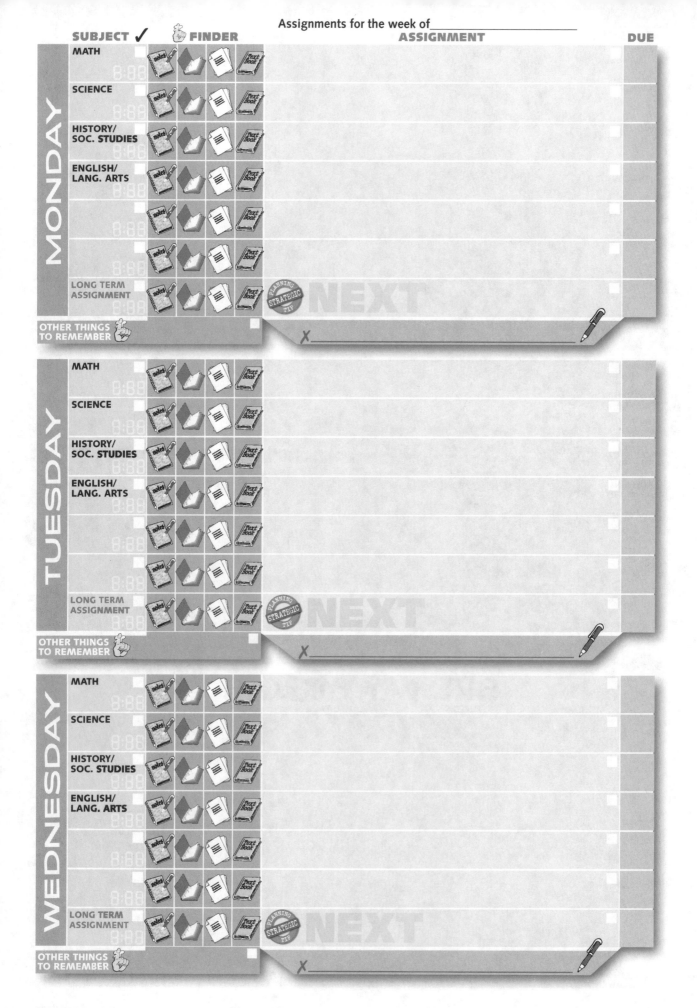

SUBJECT ✓   FINDER   ASSIGNMENT   DUE

MONDAY

MATH

SCIENCE

HISTORY/ SOC. STUDIES

ENGLISH/ LANG. ARTS

LONG TERM ASSIGNMENT

NEXT

OTHER THINGS TO REMEMBER

X_____

TUESDAY

MATH

SCIENCE

HISTORY/ SOC. STUDIES

ENGLISH/ LANG. ARTS

LONG TERM ASSIGNMENT

NEXT

OTHER THINGS TO REMEMBER

X_____

WEDNESDAY

MATH

SCIENCE

HISTORY/ SOC. STUDIES

ENGLISH/ LANG. ARTS

LONG TERM ASSIGNMENT

NEXT

OTHER THINGS TO REMEMBER

X_____

PLANNING STRATEGIC TIP

SUBJECT ✓	🐾 FINDER	ASSIGNMENT	DUE

THURSDAY

MATH	notes			Text Book		
8:88						
SCIENCE	notes			Text Book		
8:88						
HISTORY/ SOC. STUDIES	notes			Text Book		
8:88						
ENGLISH/ LANG. ARTS	notes			Text Book		
8:88						
	notes			Text Book		
8:88						
	notes			Text Book		
8:88						
LONG TERM ASSIGNMENT	notes			Text Book		
8:88						

OTHER THINGS TO REMEMBER

STRATEGIC PLANNING TIP — NEXT

X _____

FRIDAY

MATH	notes			Text Book		
8:88						
SCIENCE	notes			Text Book		
8:88						
HISTORY/ SOC. STUDIES	notes			Text Book		
8:88						
ENGLISH/ LANG. ARTS	notes			Text Book		
8:88						
	notes			Text Book		
8:88						
	notes			Text Book		
8:88						
LONG TERM ASSIGNMENT	notes			Text Book		
8:88						

OTHER THINGS TO REMEMBER

STRATEGIC PLANNING TIP — NEXT

X _____

FIVE DAY FORECAST

	MONDAY	TUESDAY	WEDNESDAY	THURSDAY	FRIDAY
BEFORE SCHOOL					
DURING SCHOOL					
AFTER SCHOOL					
EVENING					
BEFORE BED					
Homework	READY TO GO	READY TO GO	READY TO GO	READY TO GO	READY TO GO

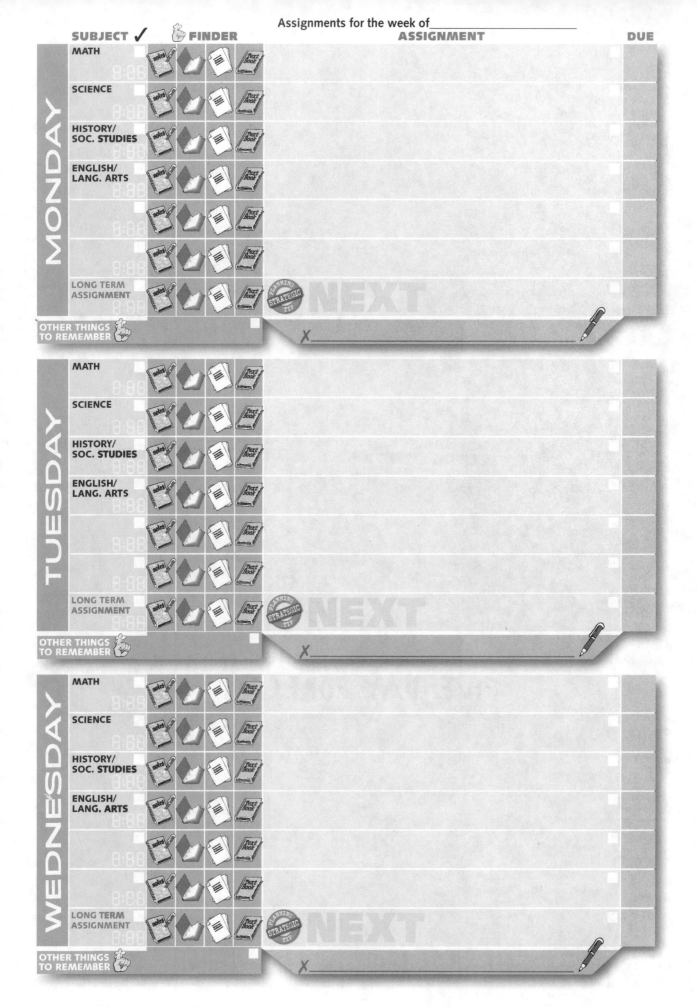

Assignments for the week of_____

SUBJECT ✓	FINDER	ASSIGNMENT	DUE

MONDAY
- MATH
- SCIENCE
- HISTORY/ SOC. STUDIES
- ENGLISH/ LANG. ARTS
- LONG TERM ASSIGNMENT

OTHER THINGS TO REMEMBER

TUESDAY
- MATH
- SCIENCE
- HISTORY/ SOC. STUDIES
- ENGLISH/ LANG. ARTS
- LONG TERM ASSIGNMENT

OTHER THINGS TO REMEMBER

WEDNESDAY
- MATH
- SCIENCE
- HISTORY/ SOC. STUDIES
- ENGLISH/ LANG. ARTS
- LONG TERM ASSIGNMENT

OTHER THINGS TO REMEMBER

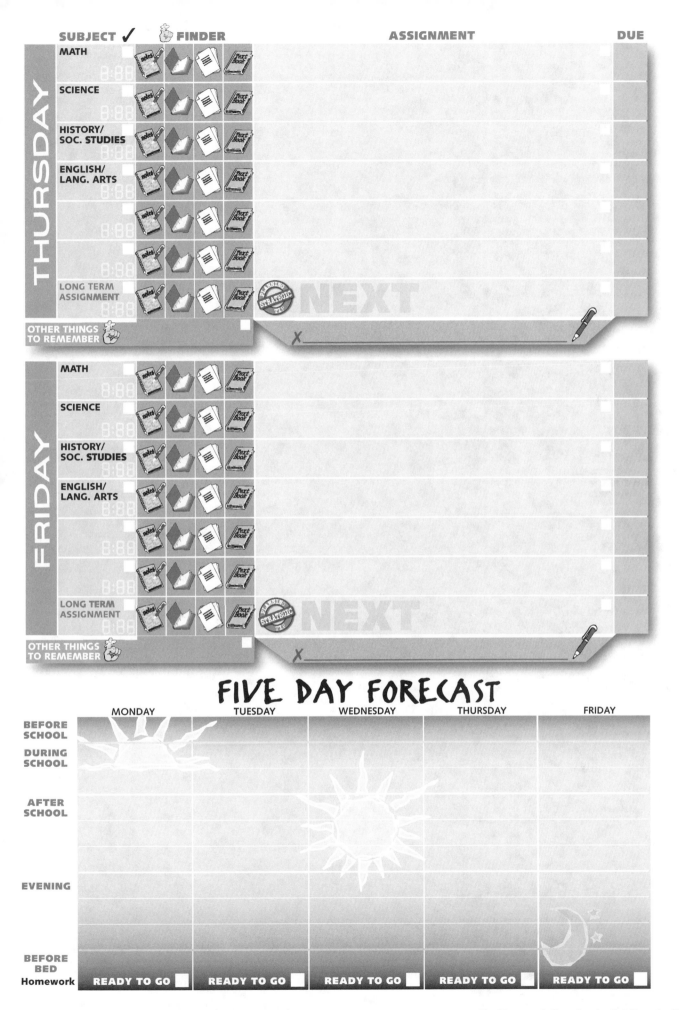

SUBJECT ✓	FINDER	ASSIGNMENT	DUE

THURSDAY

- MATH
- SCIENCE
- HISTORY/ SOC. STUDIES
- ENGLISH/ LANG. ARTS
- LONG TERM ASSIGNMENT

OTHER THINGS TO REMEMBER

NEXT

FRIDAY

- MATH
- SCIENCE
- HISTORY/ SOC. STUDIES
- ENGLISH/ LANG. ARTS
- LONG TERM ASSIGNMENT

OTHER THINGS TO REMEMBER

NEXT

FIVE DAY FORECAST

	MONDAY	TUESDAY	WEDNESDAY	THURSDAY	FRIDAY
BEFORE SCHOOL					
DURING SCHOOL					
AFTER SCHOOL					
EVENING					
BEFORE BED					
Homework	READY TO GO	READY TO GO	READY TO GO	READY TO GO	READY TO GO

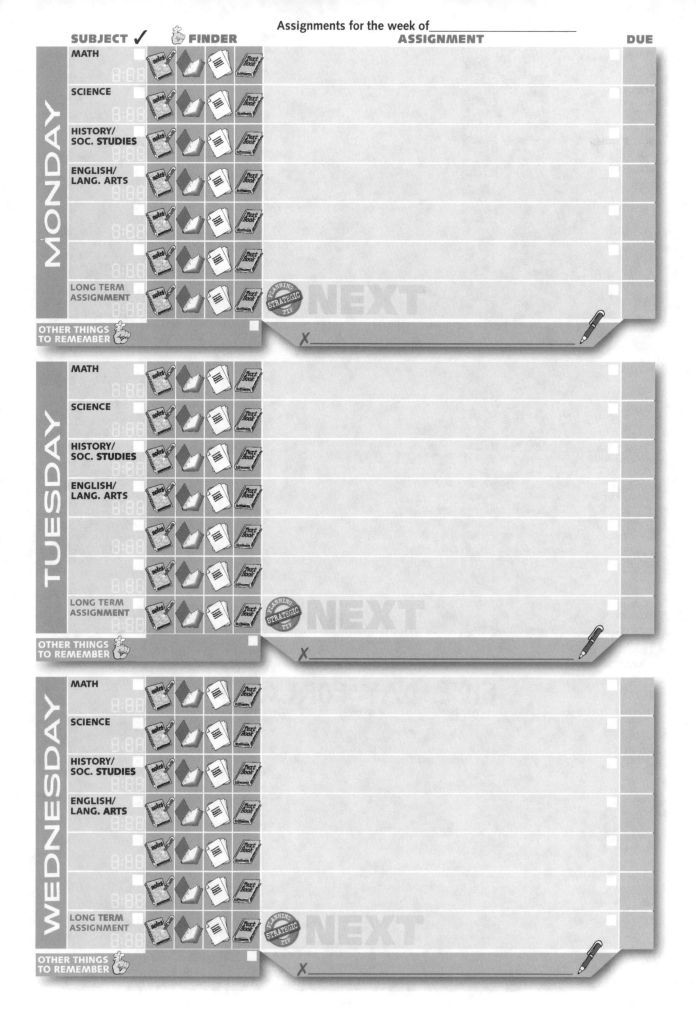

Assignments for the week of _____

SUBJECT ✓	FINDER	ASSIGNMENT	DUE

MONDAY
- MATH
- SCIENCE
- HISTORY/ SOC. STUDIES
- ENGLISH/ LANG. ARTS
- LONG TERM ASSIGNMENT

OTHER THINGS TO REMEMBER

PLANNING STRATEGIC TIP — NEXT

TUESDAY
- MATH
- SCIENCE
- HISTORY/ SOC. STUDIES
- ENGLISH/ LANG. ARTS
- LONG TERM ASSIGNMENT

OTHER THINGS TO REMEMBER

PLANNING STRATEGIC TIP — NEXT

WEDNESDAY
- MATH
- SCIENCE
- HISTORY/ SOC. STUDIES
- ENGLISH/ LANG. ARTS
- LONG TERM ASSIGNMENT

OTHER THINGS TO REMEMBER

PLANNING STRATEGIC TIP — NEXT

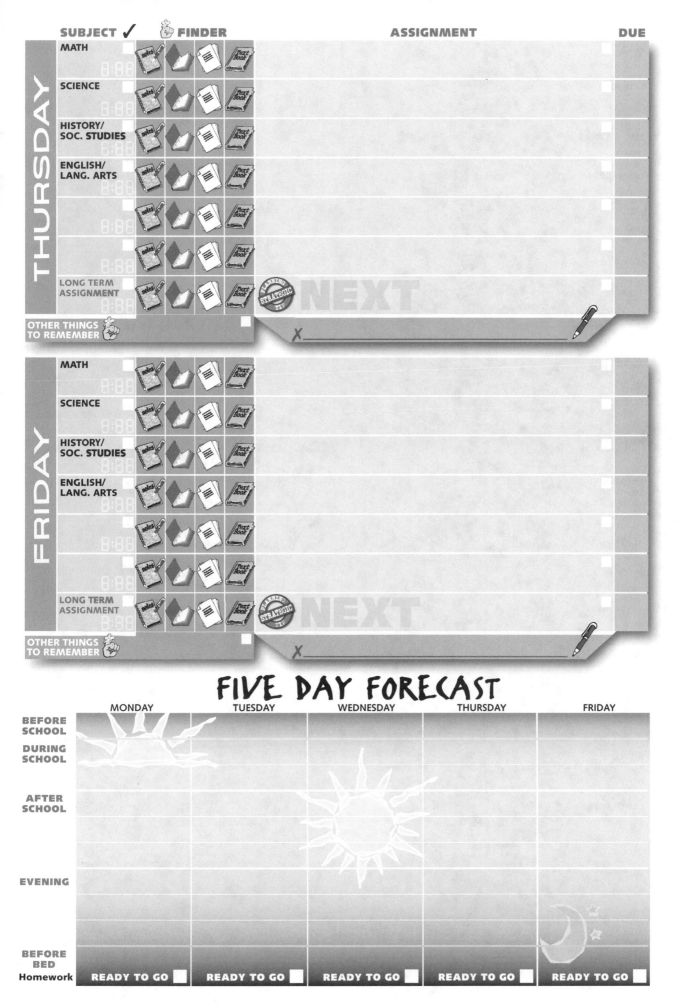

SUBJECT ✓	👆 FINDER	ASSIGNMENT	DUE

THURSDAY

MATH

SCIENCE

HISTORY/ SOC. STUDIES

ENGLISH/ LANG. ARTS

LONG TERM ASSIGNMENT

NEXT

OTHER THINGS TO REMEMBER

X _____

FRIDAY

MATH

SCIENCE

HISTORY/ SOC. STUDIES

ENGLISH/ LANG. ARTS

LONG TERM ASSIGNMENT

NEXT

OTHER THINGS TO REMEMBER

X _____

FIVE DAY FORECAST

	MONDAY	TUESDAY	WEDNESDAY	THURSDAY	FRIDAY
BEFORE SCHOOL					
DURING SCHOOL					
AFTER SCHOOL					
EVENING					
BEFORE BED					
Homework	READY TO GO	READY TO GO	READY TO GO	READY TO GO	READY TO GO

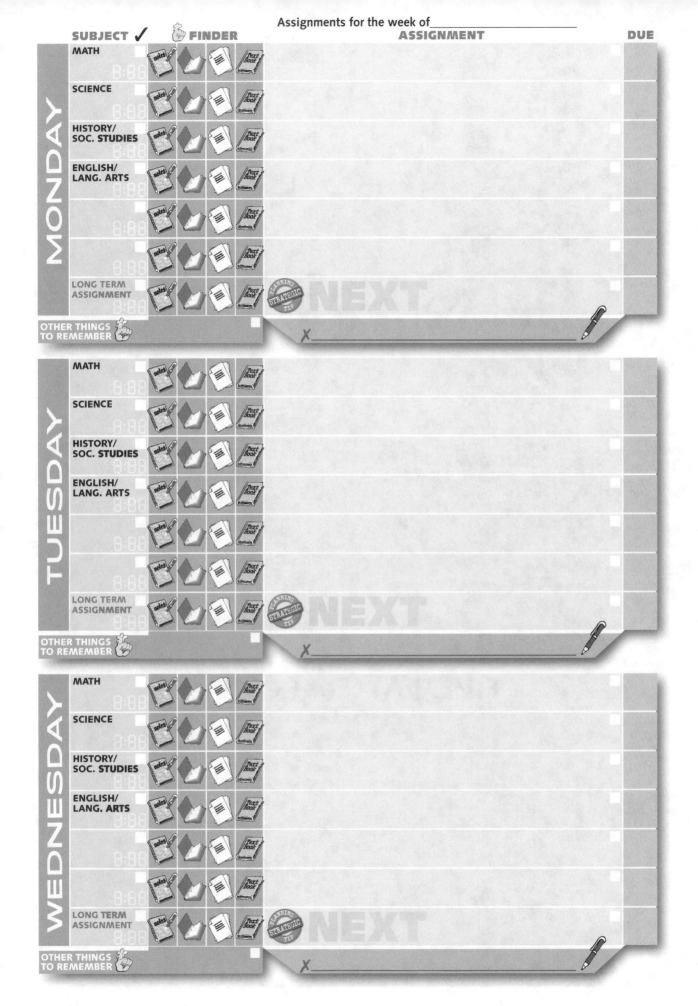

SUBJECT ✓	🔖 FINDER	ASSIGNMENT	DUE

THURSDAY

MATH	📓📔📄📕		
SCIENCE	📓📔📄📕		
HISTORY/ SOC. STUDIES	📓📔📄📕		
ENGLISH/ LANG. ARTS	📓📔📄📕		
	📓📔📄📕		
	📓📔📄📕		
LONG TERM ASSIGNMENT	📓📔📄📕 STRATEGIC	NEXT	

OTHER THINGS TO REMEMBER ✊

X_____

FRIDAY

MATH	📓📔📄📕		
SCIENCE	📓📔📄📕		
HISTORY/ SOC. STUDIES	📓📔📄📕		
ENGLISH/ LANG. ARTS	📓📔📄📕		
	📓📔📄📕		
	📓📔📄📕		
LONG TERM ASSIGNMENT	📓📔📄📕 STRATEGIC	NEXT	

OTHER THINGS TO REMEMBER ✊

X_____

FIVE DAY FORECAST

	MONDAY	TUESDAY	WEDNESDAY	THURSDAY	FRIDAY
BEFORE SCHOOL					
DURING SCHOOL					
AFTER SCHOOL					
EVENING					
BEFORE BED					
Homework	READY TO GO ☐	READY TO GO ☐	READY TO GO ☐	READY TO GO ☐	READY TO GO ☐

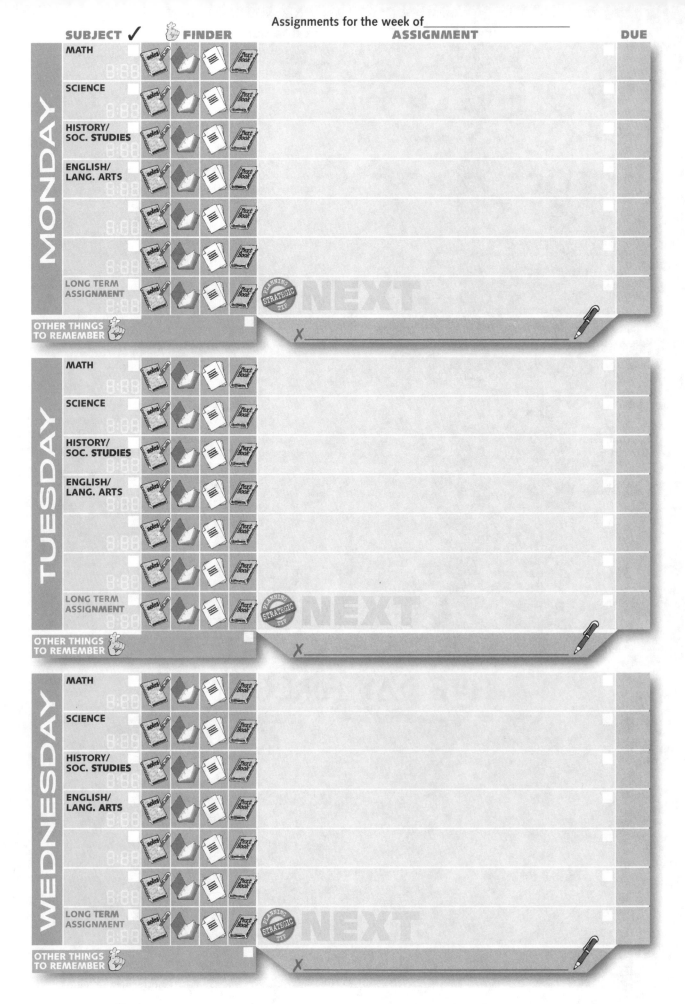

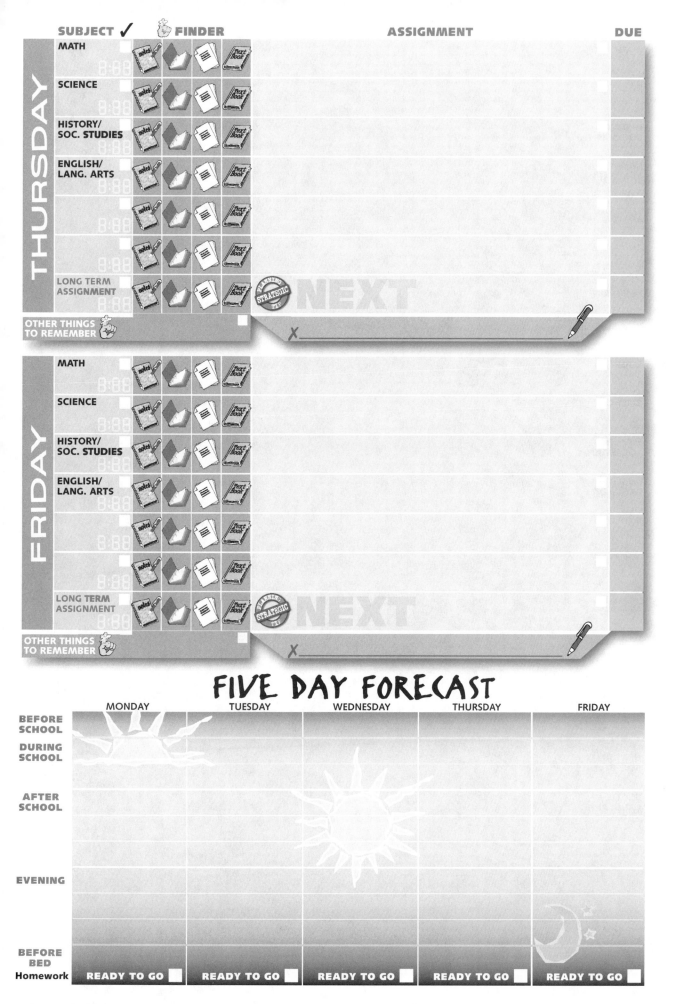

SUBJECT ✓	🐾 FINDER	ASSIGNMENT	DUE

THURSDAY

MATH			
SCIENCE			
HISTORY/ SOC. STUDIES			
ENGLISH/ LANG. ARTS			
LONG TERM ASSIGNMENT		NEXT	

OTHER THINGS TO REMEMBER

X _____

FRIDAY

MATH			
SCIENCE			
HISTORY/ SOC. STUDIES			
ENGLISH/ LANG. ARTS			
LONG TERM ASSIGNMENT		NEXT	

OTHER THINGS TO REMEMBER

X _____

FIVE DAY FORECAST

	MONDAY	TUESDAY	WEDNESDAY	THURSDAY	FRIDAY
BEFORE SCHOOL					
DURING SCHOOL					
AFTER SCHOOL					
EVENING					
BEFORE BED					
Homework	READY TO GO	READY TO GO	READY TO GO	READY TO GO	READY TO GO

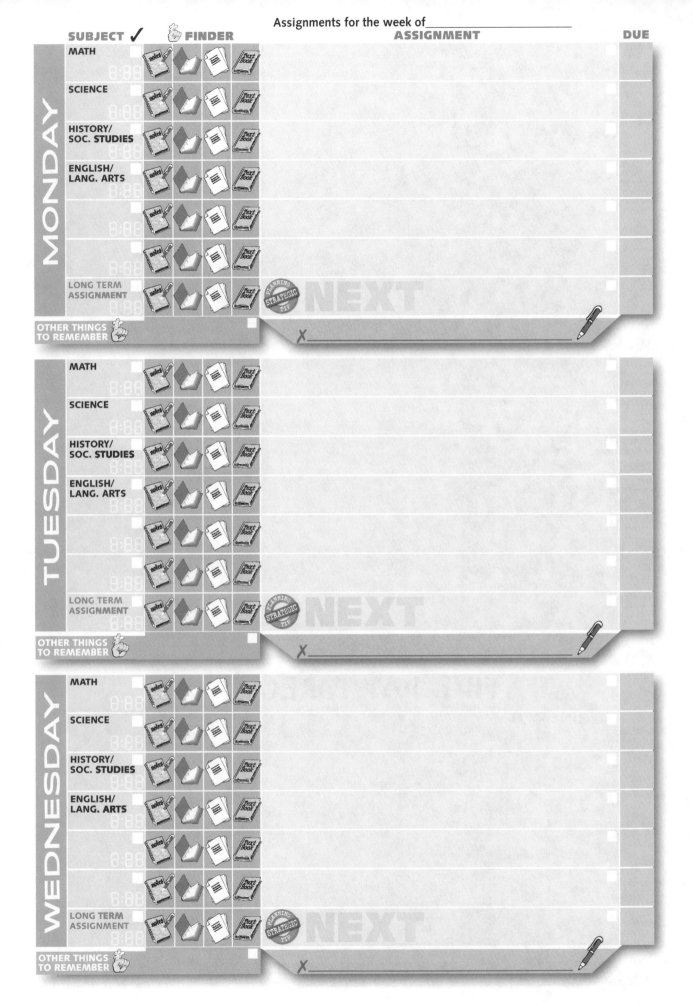

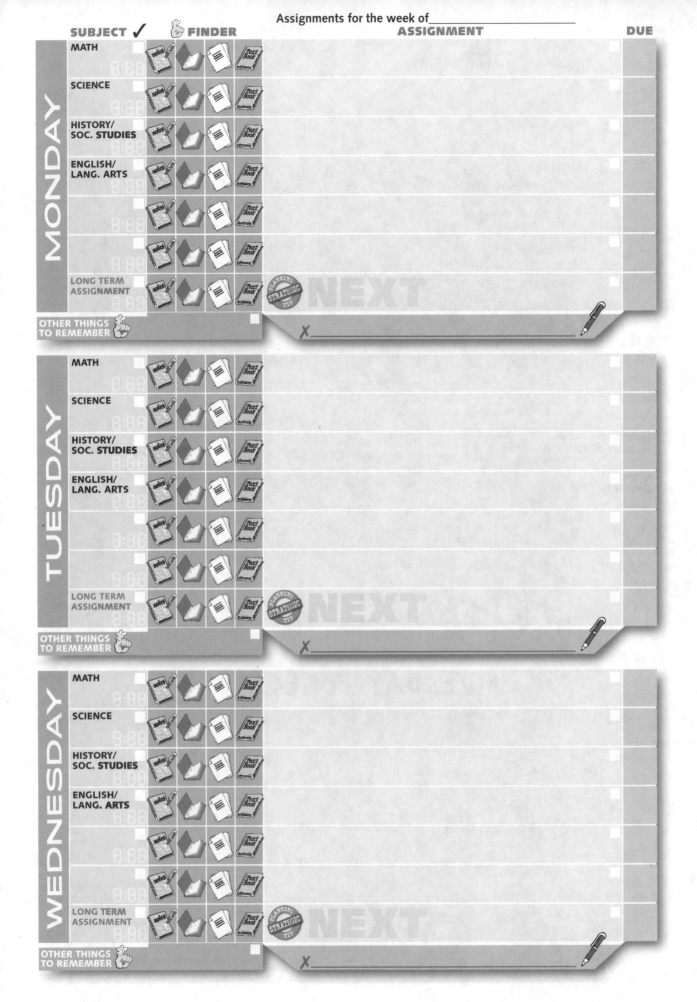

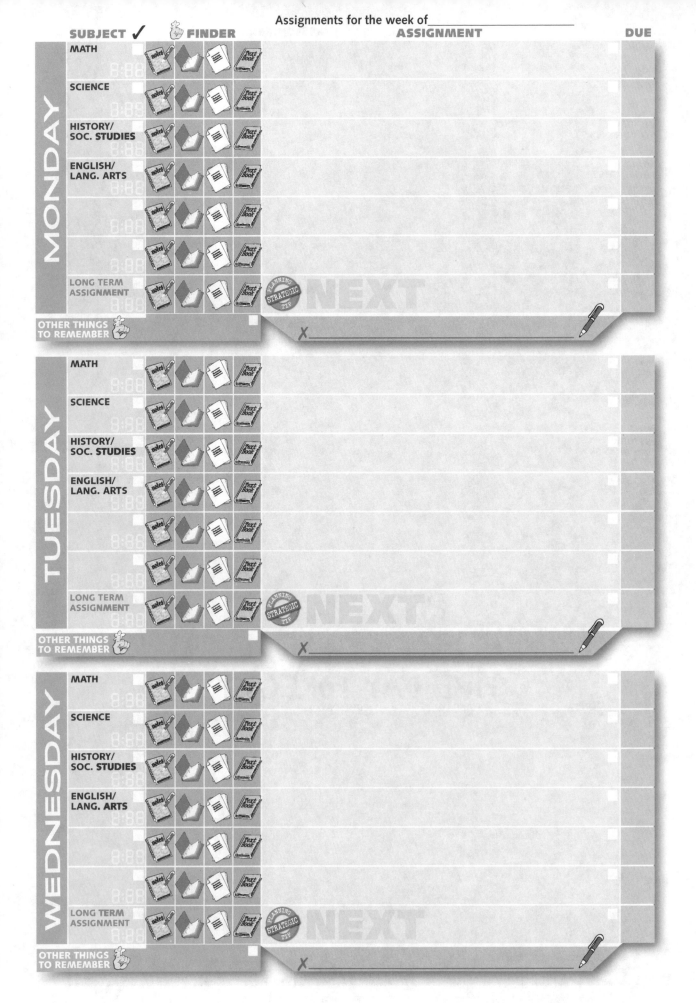

Assignments for the week of_____

SUBJECT ✓	FINDER	ASSIGNMENT	DUE

MONDAY
- MATH
- SCIENCE
- HISTORY/ SOC. STUDIES
- ENGLISH/ LANG. ARTS
- LONG TERM ASSIGNMENT

OTHER THINGS TO REMEMBER

TUESDAY
- MATH
- SCIENCE
- HISTORY/ SOC. STUDIES
- ENGLISH/ LANG. ARTS
- LONG TERM ASSIGNMENT

OTHER THINGS TO REMEMBER

WEDNESDAY
- MATH
- SCIENCE
- HISTORY/ SOC. STUDIES
- ENGLISH/ LANG. ARTS
- LONG TERM ASSIGNMENT

OTHER THINGS TO REMEMBER

PLANNING STRATEGIC TIP — NEXT

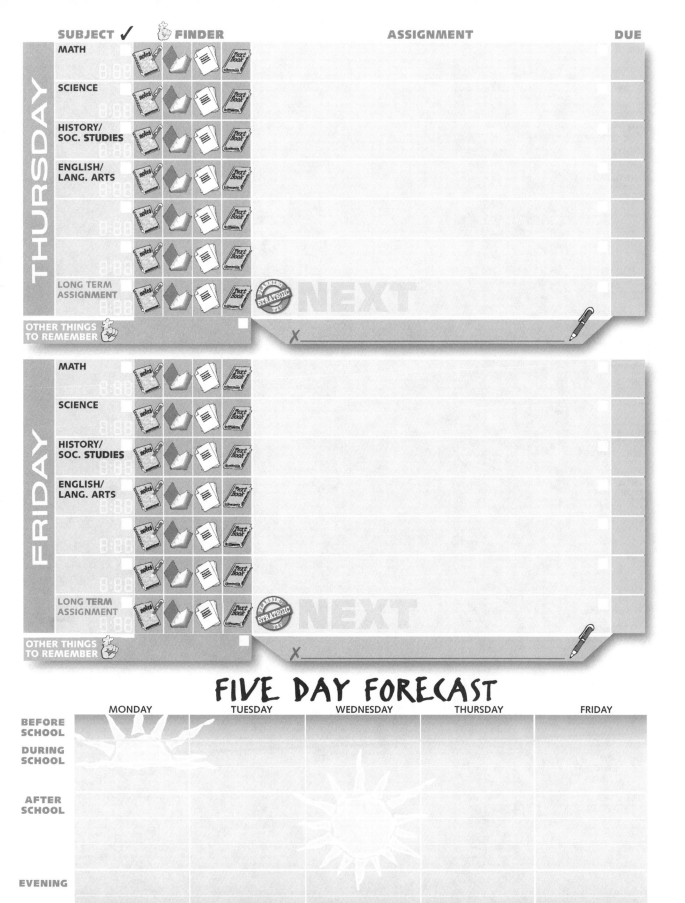

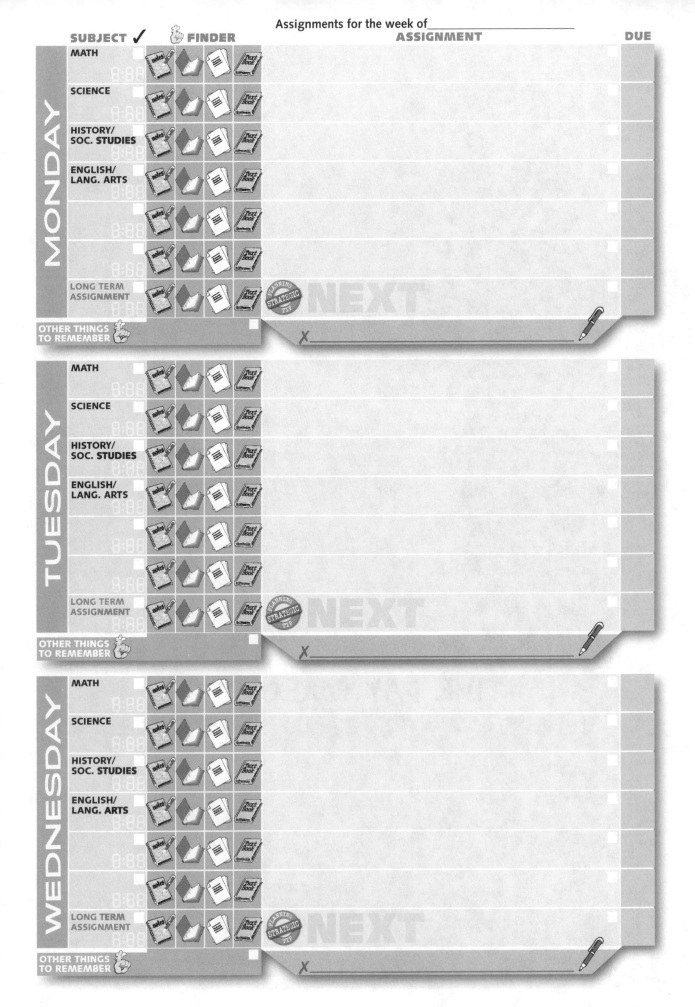

Assignments for the week of_____

SUBJECT ✓   **FINDER**   **ASSIGNMENT**   **DUE**

MONDAY

- MATH
- SCIENCE
- HISTORY/ SOC. STUDIES
- ENGLISH/ LANG. ARTS
- LONG TERM ASSIGNMENT

OTHER THINGS TO REMEMBER

TUESDAY

- MATH
- SCIENCE
- HISTORY/ SOC. STUDIES
- ENGLISH/ LANG. ARTS
- LONG TERM ASSIGNMENT

OTHER THINGS TO REMEMBER

WEDNESDAY

- MATH
- SCIENCE
- HISTORY/ SOC. STUDIES
- ENGLISH/ LANG. ARTS
- LONG TERM ASSIGNMENT

OTHER THINGS TO REMEMBER

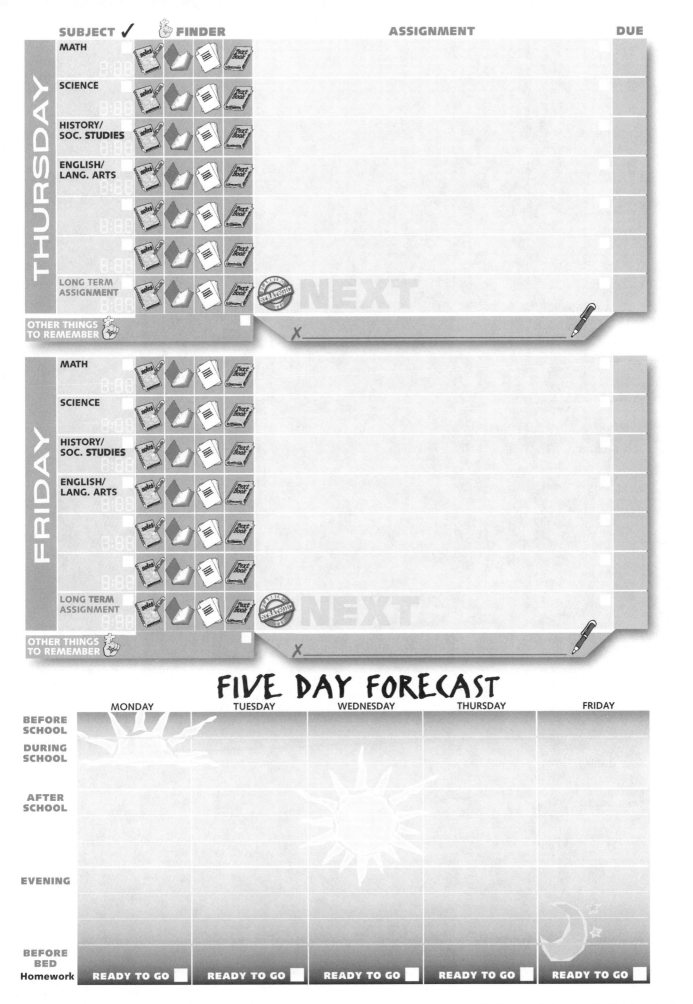

SUBJECT ✓	👆 FINDER	ASSIGNMENT	DUE

THURSDAY

MATH	notes			Text Book		
SCIENCE	notes			Text Book		
HISTORY/ SOC. STUDIES	notes			Text Book		
ENGLISH/ LANG. ARTS	notes			Text Book		
	notes			Text Book		
	notes			Text Book		
LONG TERM ASSIGNMENT	notes			Text Book	NEXT	

PLANNING STRATEGIC TIP

OTHER THINGS TO REMEMBER 👆

X _____

FRIDAY

MATH	notes			Text Book		
SCIENCE	notes			Text Book		
HISTORY/ SOC. STUDIES	notes			Text Book		
ENGLISH/ LANG. ARTS	notes			Text Book		
	notes			Text Book		
	notes			Text Book		
LONG TERM ASSIGNMENT	notes			Text Book	NEXT	

PLANNING STRATEGIC TIP

OTHER THINGS TO REMEMBER 👆

X _____

FIVE DAY FORECAST

	MONDAY	TUESDAY	WEDNESDAY	THURSDAY	FRIDAY
BEFORE SCHOOL					
DURING SCHOOL					
AFTER SCHOOL					
EVENING					
BEFORE BED					
Homework	READY TO GO	READY TO GO	READY TO GO	READY TO GO	READY TO GO

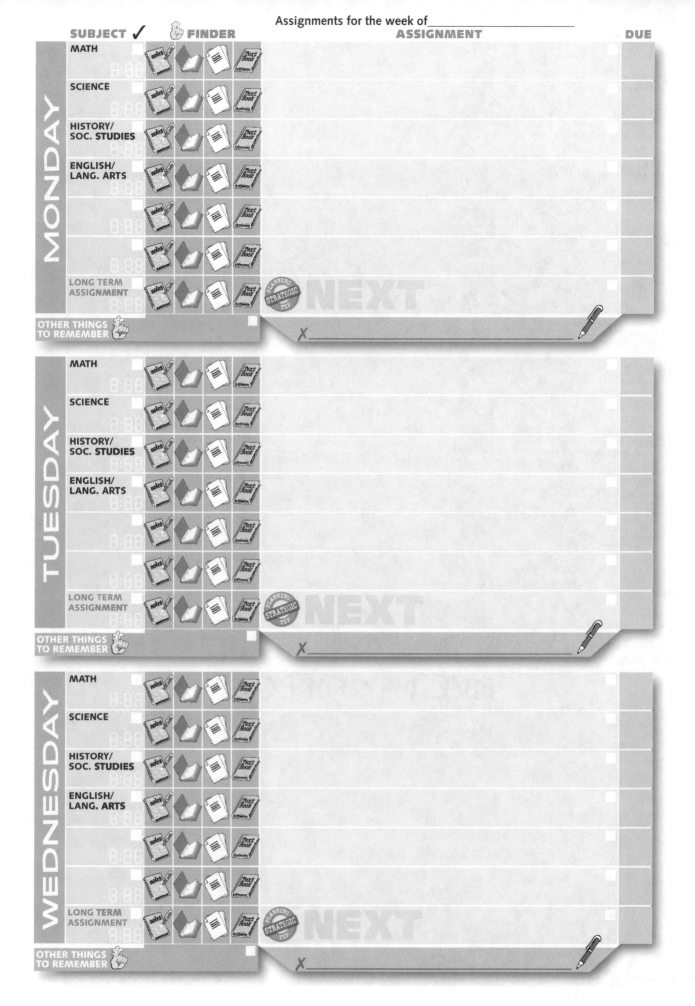

SUBJECT ✓	FINDER	ASSIGNMENT	DUE
THURSDAY			
MATH			
SCIENCE			
HISTORY/ SOC. STUDIES			
ENGLISH/ LANG. ARTS			
LONG TERM ASSIGNMENT		NEXT	
OTHER THINGS TO REMEMBER		X _____	

SUBJECT ✓	FINDER	ASSIGNMENT	DUE
FRIDAY			
MATH			
SCIENCE			
HISTORY/ SOC. STUDIES			
ENGLISH/ LANG. ARTS			
LONG TERM ASSIGNMENT		NEXT	
OTHER THINGS TO REMEMBER		X _____	

FIVE DAY FORECAST

	MONDAY	TUESDAY	WEDNESDAY	THURSDAY	FRIDAY
BEFORE SCHOOL					
DURING SCHOOL					
AFTER SCHOOL					
EVENING					
BEFORE BED Homework	READY TO GO	READY TO GO	READY TO GO	READY TO GO	READY TO GO

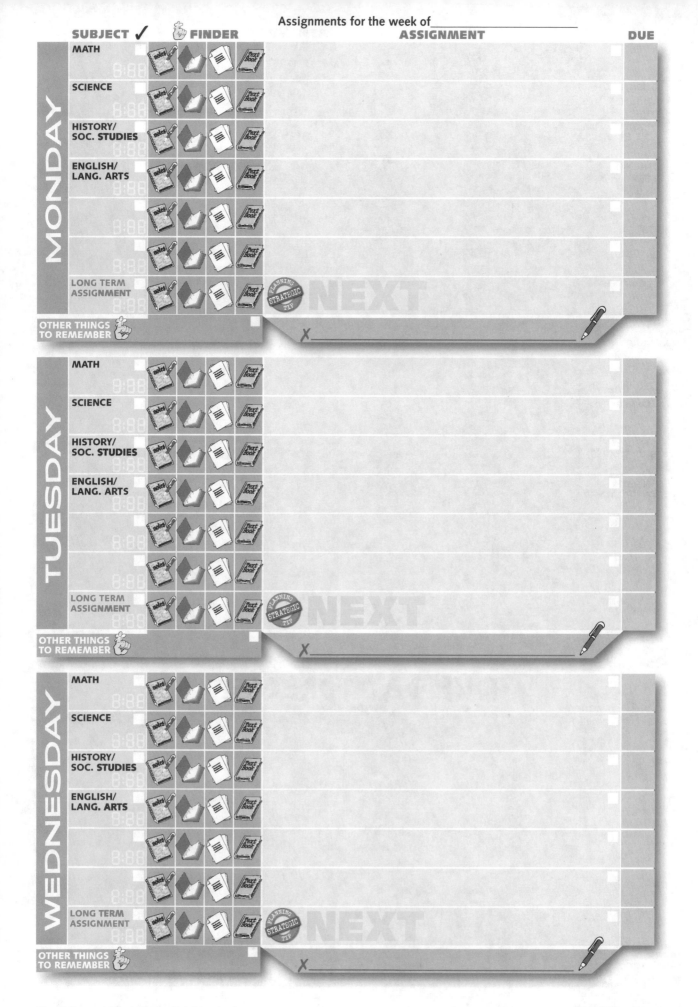

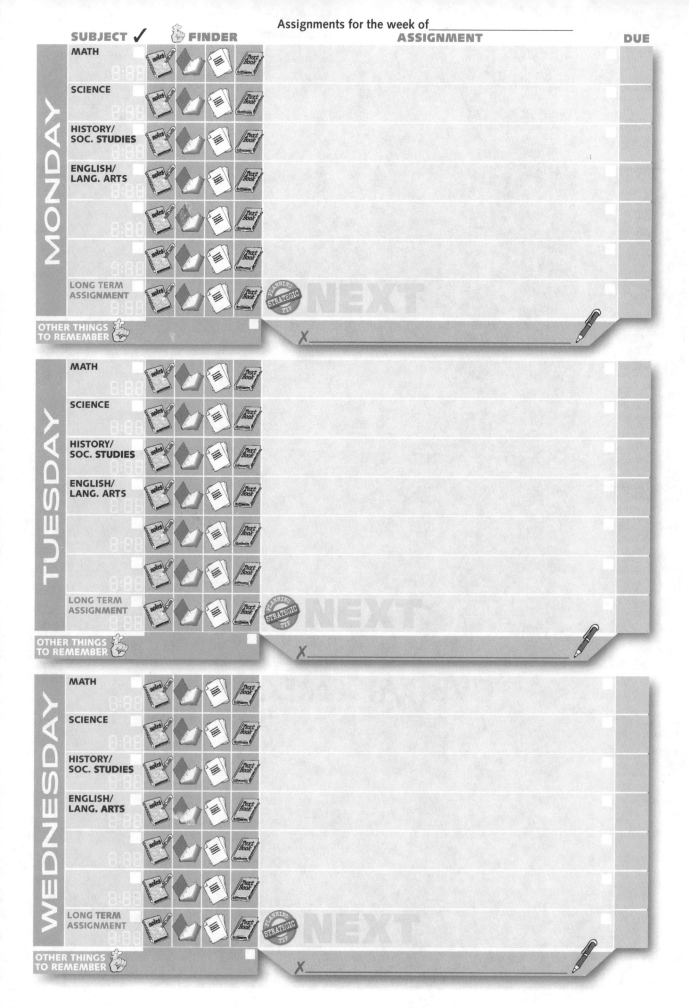

Assignments for the week of_____

SUBJECT ✓	FINDER	ASSIGNMENT	DUE

MONDAY
- MATH
- SCIENCE
- HISTORY/SOC. STUDIES
- ENGLISH/LANG. ARTS
- LONG TERM ASSIGNMENT

OTHER THINGS TO REMEMBER

TUESDAY
- MATH
- SCIENCE
- HISTORY/SOC. STUDIES
- ENGLISH/LANG. ARTS
- LONG TERM ASSIGNMENT

OTHER THINGS TO REMEMBER

WEDNESDAY
- MATH
- SCIENCE
- HISTORY/SOC. STUDIES
- ENGLISH/LANG. ARTS
- LONG TERM ASSIGNMENT

OTHER THINGS TO REMEMBER

NEXT — PLANNING STRATEGIC TIP

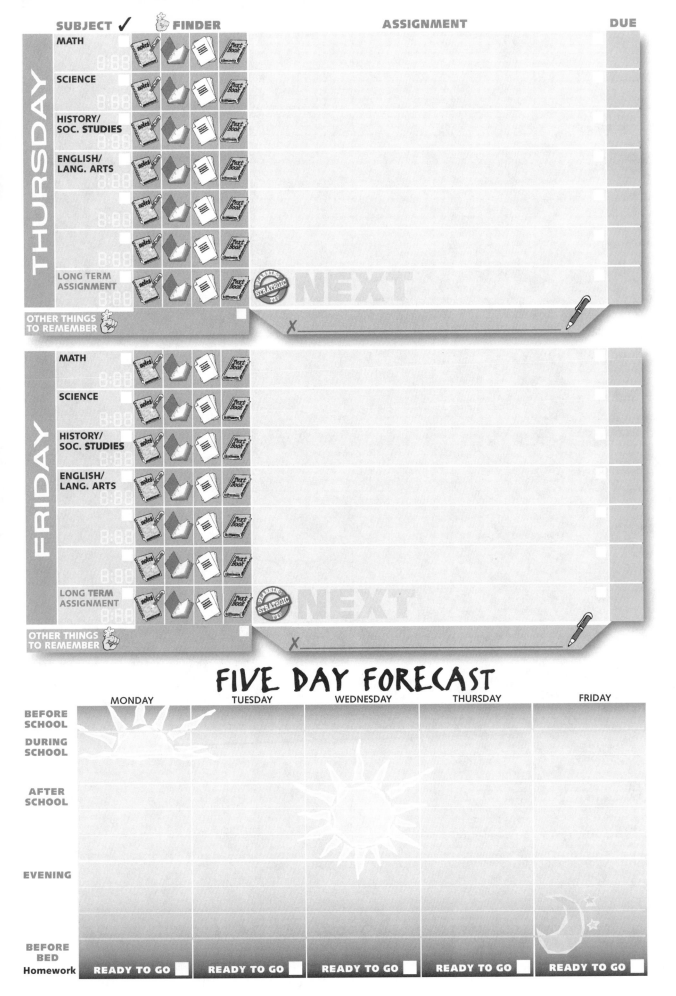

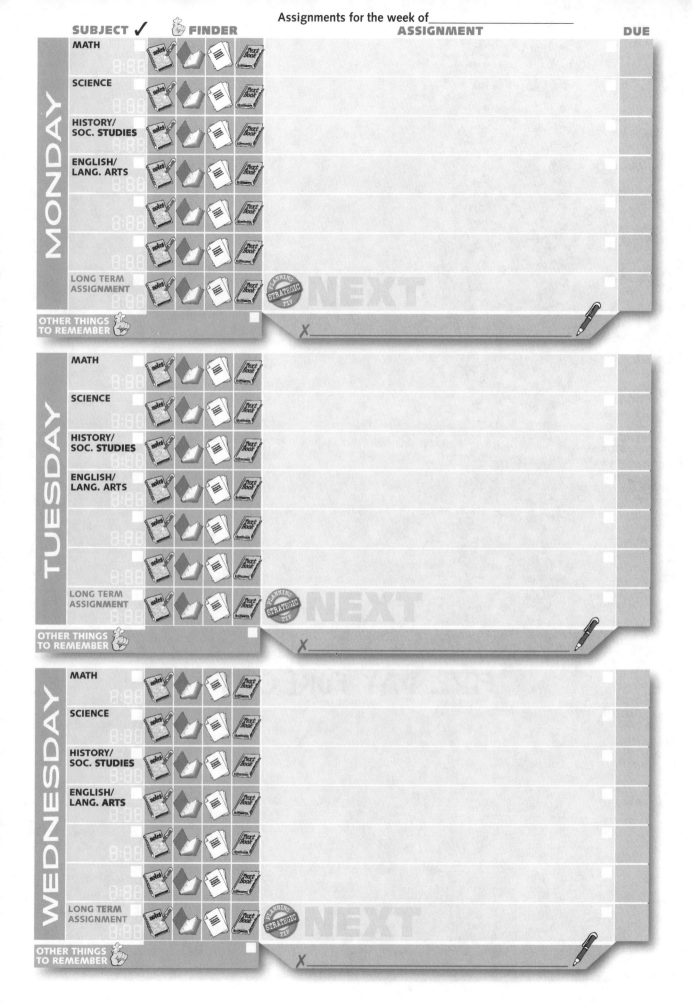

SUBJECT ✓ 🍳FINDER ASSIGNMENT DUE

THURSDAY

MATH						
SCIENCE						
HISTORY/ SOC. STUDIES						
ENGLISH/ LANG. ARTS						
LONG TERM ASSIGNMENT						

PLANNING STRATEGIC TIP — NEXT

OTHER THINGS TO REMEMBER

X _____

FRIDAY

MATH						
SCIENCE						
HISTORY/ SOC. STUDIES						
ENGLISH/ LANG. ARTS						
LONG TERM ASSIGNMENT						

PLANNING STRATEGIC TIP — NEXT

OTHER THINGS TO REMEMBER

X _____

FIVE DAY FORECAST

	MONDAY	TUESDAY	WEDNESDAY	THURSDAY	FRIDAY
BEFORE SCHOOL					
DURING SCHOOL					
AFTER SCHOOL					
EVENING					
BEFORE BED Homework	READY TO GO ☐	READY TO GO ☐	READY TO GO ☐	READY TO GO ☐	READY TO GO ☐

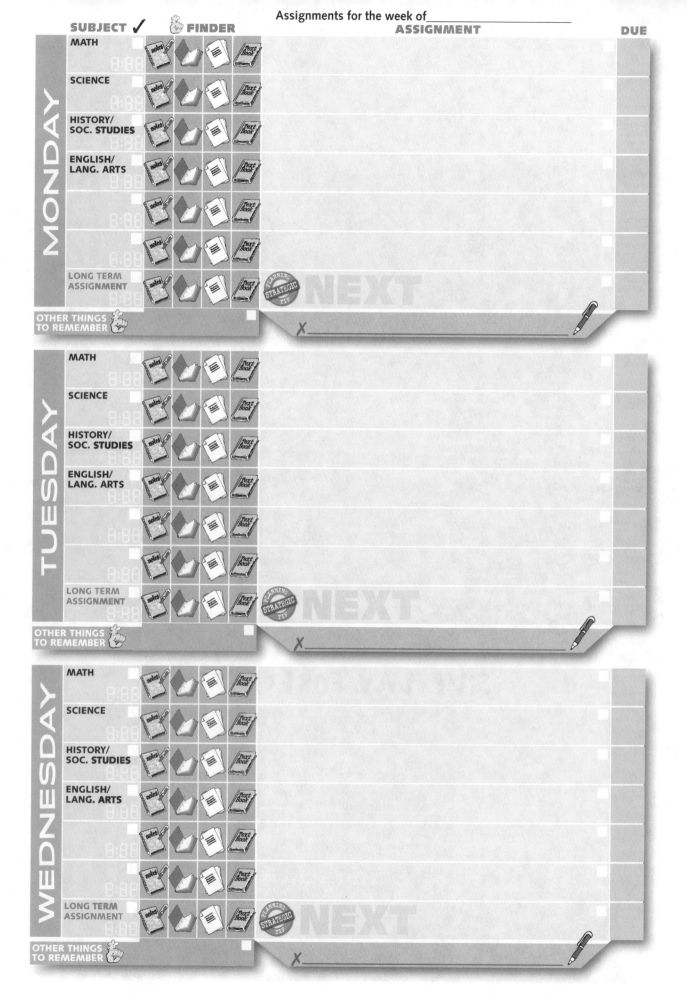

Assignments for the week of_____

SUBJECT ✓   **FINDER**   **ASSIGNMENT**   **DUE**

MONDAY
- MATH
- SCIENCE
- HISTORY/ SOC. STUDIES
- ENGLISH/ LANG. ARTS
- LONG TERM ASSIGNMENT

OTHER THINGS TO REMEMBER

TUESDAY
- MATH
- SCIENCE
- HISTORY/ SOC. STUDIES
- ENGLISH/ LANG. ARTS
- LONG TERM ASSIGNMENT

OTHER THINGS TO REMEMBER

WEDNESDAY
- MATH
- SCIENCE
- HISTORY/ SOC. STUDIES
- ENGLISH/ LANG. ARTS
- LONG TERM ASSIGNMENT

OTHER THINGS TO REMEMBER

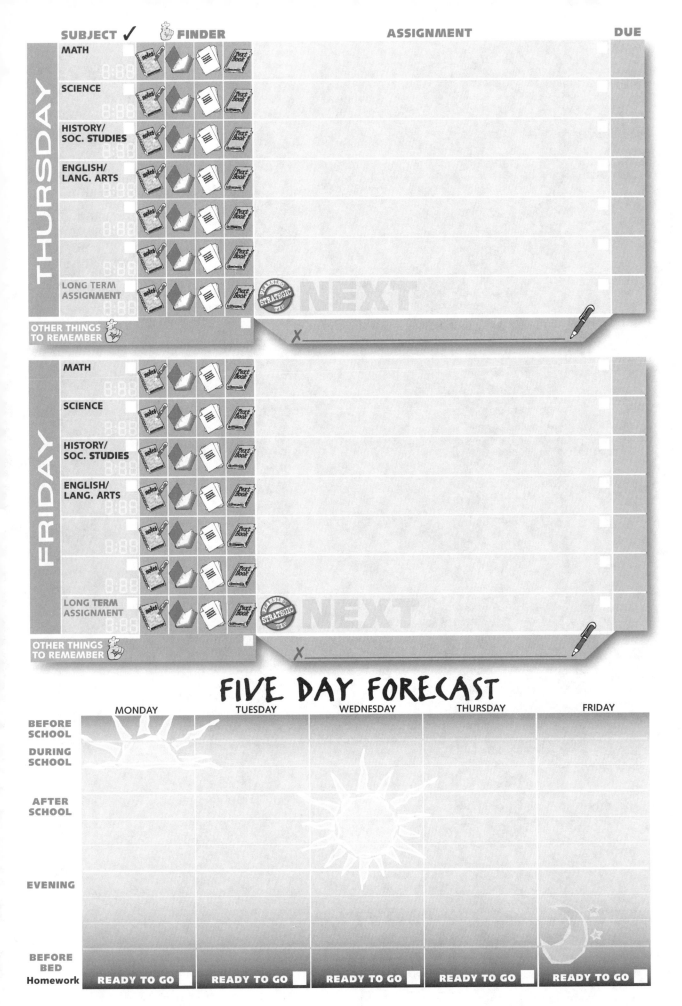

SUBJECT ✔	FINDER	ASSIGNMENT	DUE

THURSDAY

MATH			
SCIENCE			
HISTORY/ SOC. STUDIES			
ENGLISH/ LANG. ARTS			
LONG TERM ASSIGNMENT			

PLANNING STRATEGIC TIP — NEXT

OTHER THINGS TO REMEMBER

X _____

FRIDAY

MATH			
SCIENCE			
HISTORY/ SOC. STUDIES			
ENGLISH/ LANG. ARTS			
LONG TERM ASSIGNMENT			

PLANNING STRATEGIC TIP — NEXT

OTHER THINGS TO REMEMBER

X _____

FIVE DAY FORECAST

	MONDAY	TUESDAY	WEDNESDAY	THURSDAY	FRIDAY
BEFORE SCHOOL					
DURING SCHOOL					
AFTER SCHOOL					
EVENING					
BEFORE BED					
Homework	READY TO GO ☐	READY TO GO ☐	READY TO GO ☐	READY TO GO ☐	READY TO GO ☐

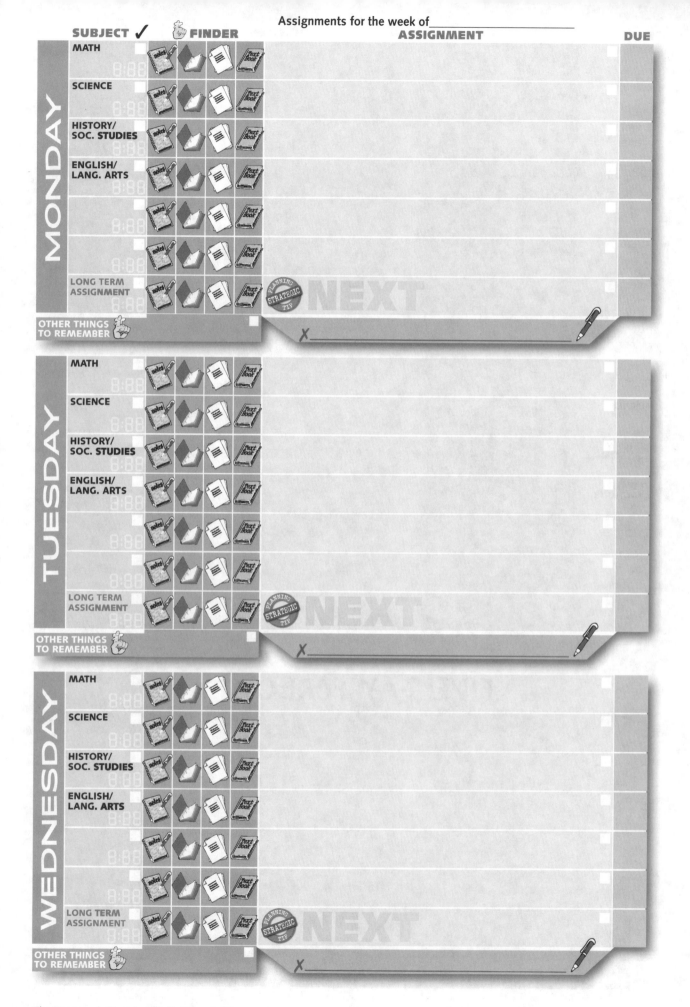

Assignments for the week of_____

SUBJECT ✓ **FINDER** **ASSIGNMENT** **DUE**

MONDAY
- MATH
- SCIENCE
- HISTORY/ SOC. STUDIES
- ENGLISH/ LANG. ARTS
- LONG TERM ASSIGNMENT

OTHER THINGS TO REMEMBER

TUESDAY
- MATH
- SCIENCE
- HISTORY/ SOC. STUDIES
- ENGLISH/ LANG. ARTS
- LONG TERM ASSIGNMENT

OTHER THINGS TO REMEMBER

WEDNESDAY
- MATH
- SCIENCE
- HISTORY/ SOC. STUDIES
- ENGLISH/ LANG. ARTS
- LONG TERM ASSIGNMENT

OTHER THINGS TO REMEMBER

NEXT

PLANNING STRATEGIC TIP

SUBJECT ✓	🖐 FINDER	ASSIGNMENT	DUE

THURSDAY

MATH			
SCIENCE			
HISTORY/ SOC. STUDIES			
ENGLISH/ LANG. ARTS			
LONG TERM ASSIGNMENT			

OTHER THINGS TO REMEMBER 🖐

PLANNING STRATEGIC TIP — NEXT

X _____

FRIDAY

MATH			
SCIENCE			
HISTORY/ SOC. STUDIES			
ENGLISH/ LANG. ARTS			
LONG TERM ASSIGNMENT			

OTHER THINGS TO REMEMBER 🖐

PLANNING STRATEGIC TIP — NEXT

X _____

FIVE DAY FORECAST

	MONDAY	TUESDAY	WEDNESDAY	THURSDAY	FRIDAY
BEFORE SCHOOL					
DURING SCHOOL					
AFTER SCHOOL					
EVENING					
BEFORE BED Homework	READY TO GO	READY TO GO	READY TO GO	READY TO GO	READY TO GO

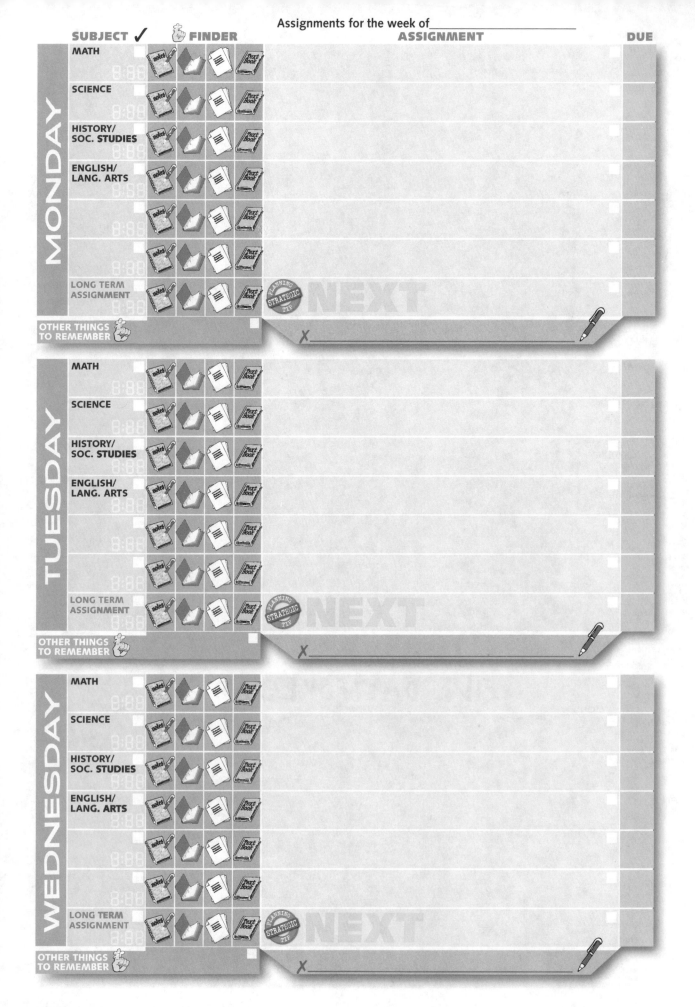

Assignments for the week of _____

SUBJECT ✓   FINDER   ASSIGNMENT   DUE

MONDAY

MATH
SCIENCE
HISTORY/ SOC. STUDIES
ENGLISH/ LANG. ARTS
LONG TERM ASSIGNMENT

OTHER THINGS TO REMEMBER

TUESDAY

MATH
SCIENCE
HISTORY/ SOC. STUDIES
ENGLISH/ LANG. ARTS
LONG TERM ASSIGNMENT

OTHER THINGS TO REMEMBER

WEDNESDAY

MATH
SCIENCE
HISTORY/ SOC. STUDIES
ENGLISH/ LANG. ARTS
LONG TERM ASSIGNMENT

OTHER THINGS TO REMEMBER

PLANNING STRATEGIC TIP — NEXT

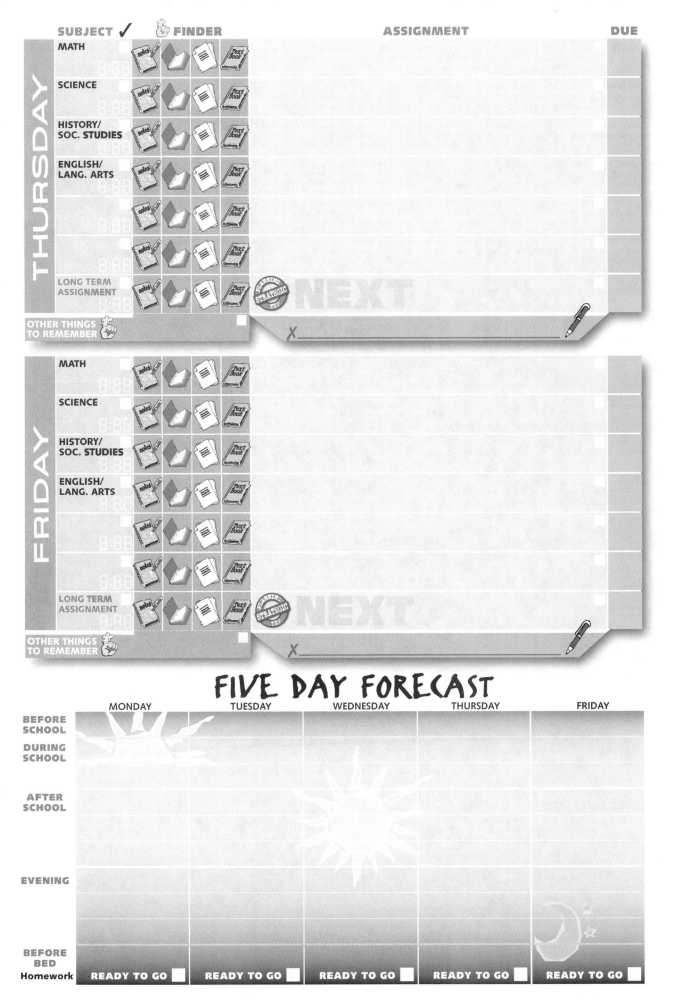

SUBJECT ✓	FINDER	ASSIGNMENT	DUE
THURSDAY			
MATH			
SCIENCE			
HISTORY/ SOC. **STUDIES**			
ENGLISH/ LANG. ARTS			
LONG TERM ASSIGNMENT		NEXT	
OTHER THINGS TO REMEMBER		X _____	

SUBJECT ✓	FINDER	ASSIGNMENT	DUE
FRIDAY			
MATH			
SCIENCE			
HISTORY/ SOC. STUDIES			
ENGLISH/ LANG. ARTS			
LONG TERM ASSIGNMENT		NEXT	
OTHER THINGS TO REMEMBER		X _____	

FIVE DAY FORECAST

	MONDAY	TUESDAY	WEDNESDAY	THURSDAY	FRIDAY
BEFORE SCHOOL					
DURING SCHOOL					
AFTER SCHOOL					
EVENING					
BEFORE BED					
Homework	READY TO GO	READY TO GO	READY TO GO	READY TO GO	READY TO GO

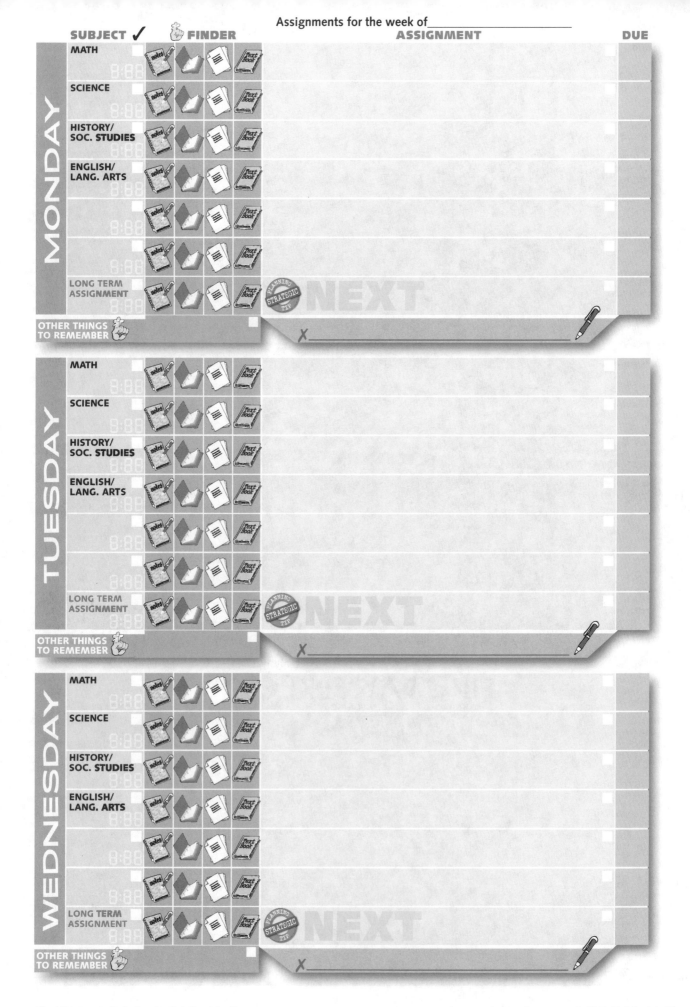

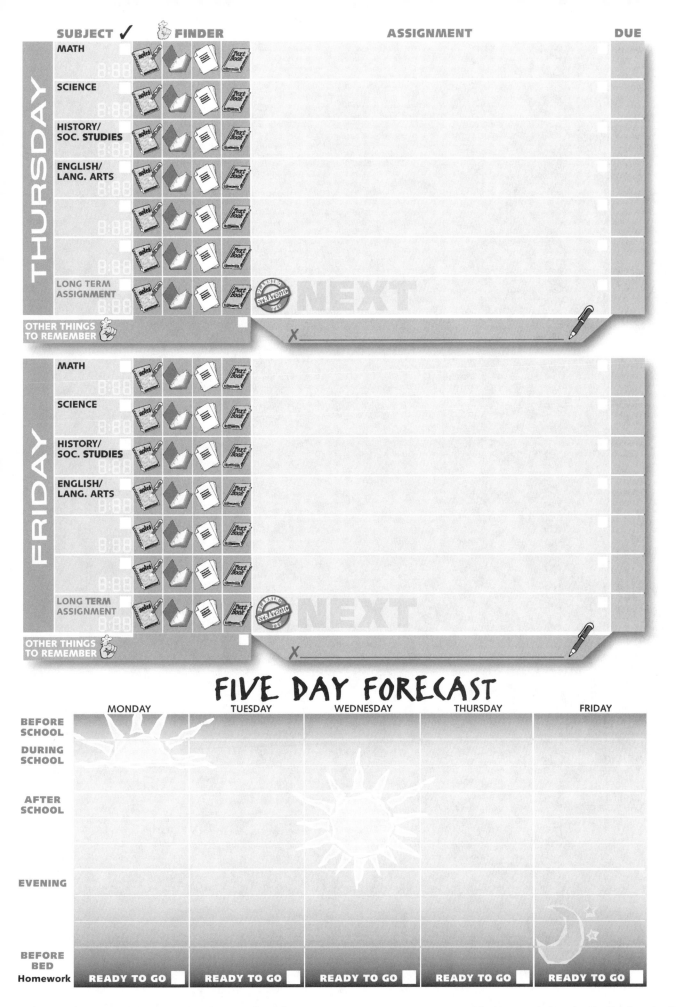

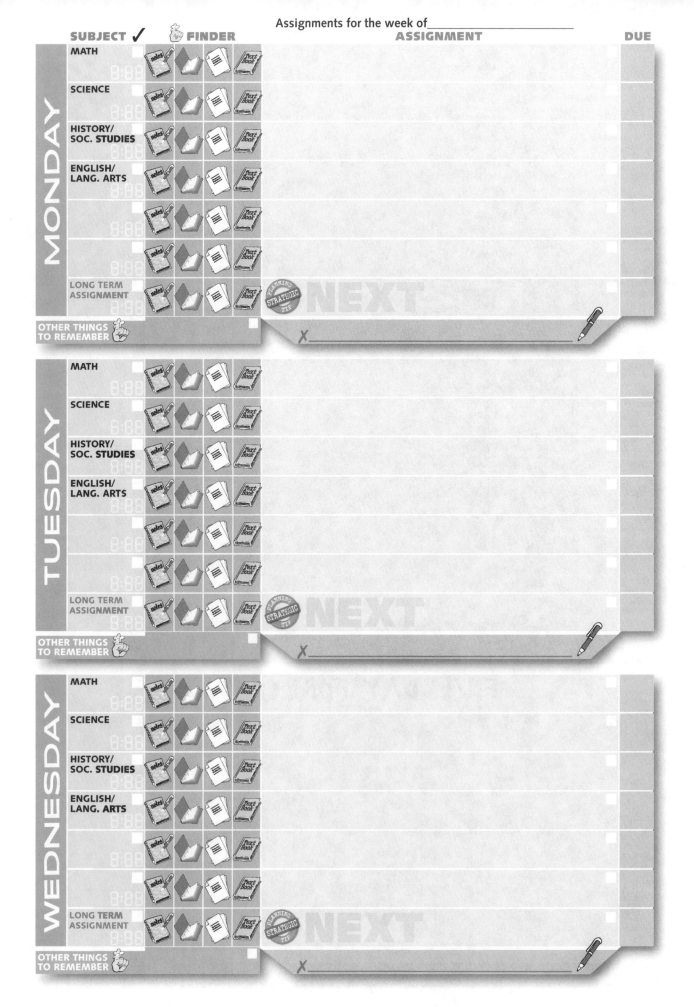

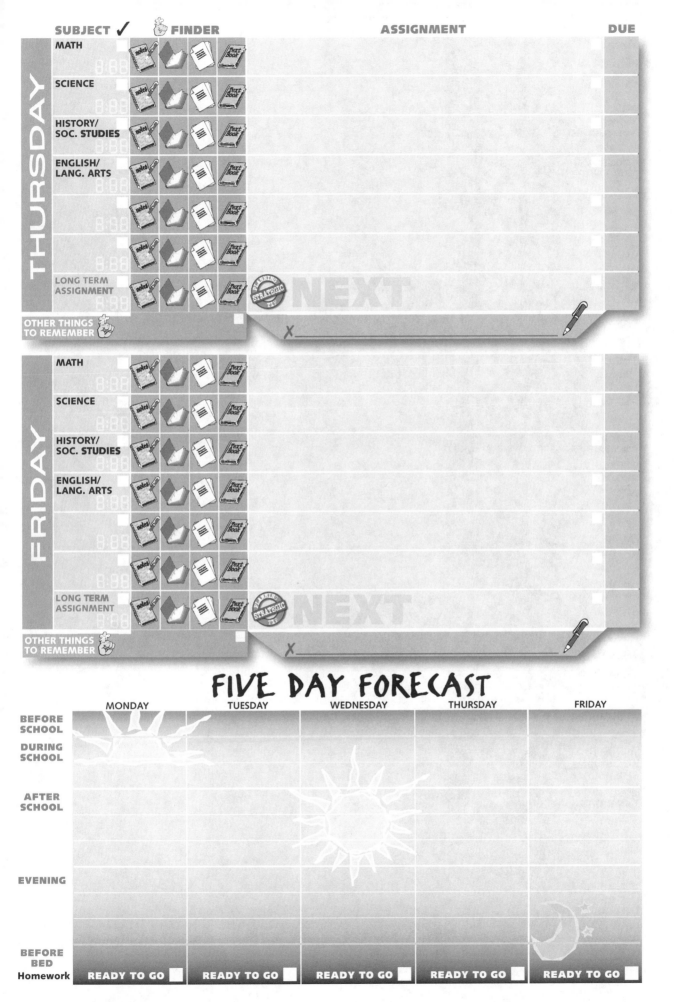

SUBJECT ✓	FINDER	ASSIGNMENT	DUE

THURSDAY

- MATH
- SCIENCE
- HISTORY/SOC. STUDIES
- ENGLISH/LANG. ARTS
- LONG TERM ASSIGNMENT

OTHER THINGS TO REMEMBER

PLANNING STRATEGIC TIP · NEXT

X _____

FRIDAY

- MATH
- SCIENCE
- HISTORY/SOC. STUDIES
- ENGLISH/LANG. ARTS
- LONG TERM ASSIGNMENT

OTHER THINGS TO REMEMBER

PLANNING STRATEGIC TIP · NEXT

X _____

FIVE DAY FORECAST

	MONDAY	TUESDAY	WEDNESDAY	THURSDAY	FRIDAY
BEFORE SCHOOL					
DURING SCHOOL					
AFTER SCHOOL					
EVENING					
BEFORE BED					
Homework	READY TO GO	READY TO GO	READY TO GO	READY TO GO	READY TO GO

Assignments for the week of_____

SUBJECT ✓	FINDER	ASSIGNMENT	DUE

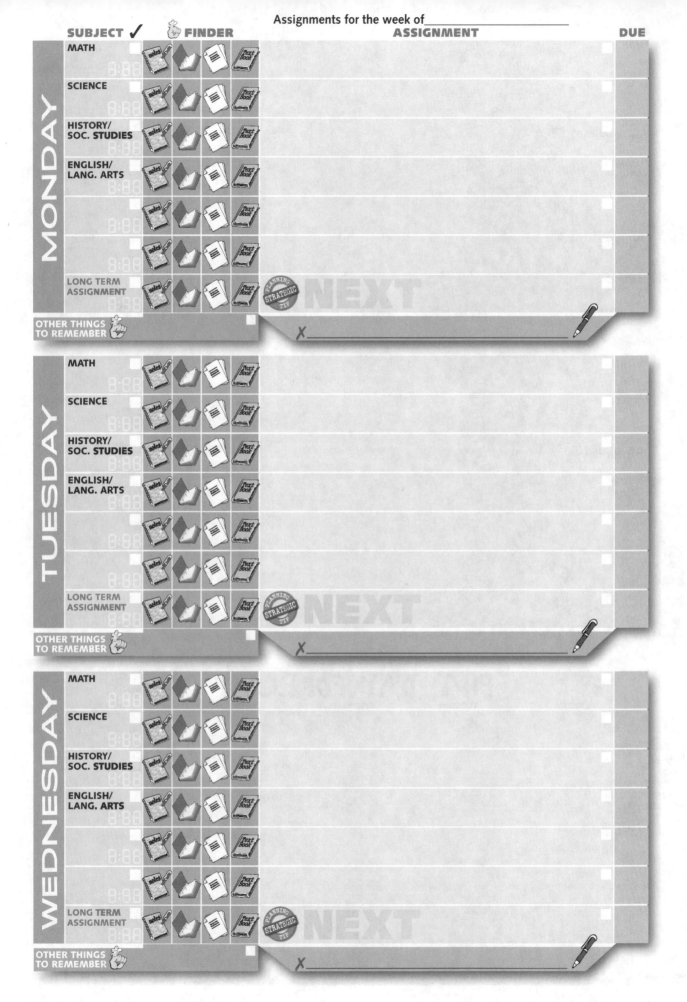

MONDAY

- MATH
- SCIENCE
- HISTORY/SOC. STUDIES
- ENGLISH/LANG. ARTS
- LONG TERM ASSIGNMENT

OTHER THINGS TO REMEMBER

NEXT

X_____

TUESDAY

- MATH
- SCIENCE
- HISTORY/SOC. STUDIES
- ENGLISH/LANG. ARTS
- LONG TERM ASSIGNMENT

OTHER THINGS TO REMEMBER

NEXT

X_____

WEDNESDAY

- MATH
- SCIENCE
- HISTORY/SOC. STUDIES
- ENGLISH/LANG. ARTS
- LONG TERM ASSIGNMENT

OTHER THINGS TO REMEMBER

NEXT

X_____

STRATEGIC PLANNING TIP

SUBJECT ✓	FINDER	ASSIGNMENT	DUE
THURSDAY			
MATH			
SCIENCE			
HISTORY/ SOC. STUDIES			
ENGLISH/ LANG. ARTS			
LONG TERM ASSIGNMENT	PLANNING STRATEGIC TIP	NEXT	
OTHER THINGS TO REMEMBER		X _____	

SUBJECT ✓	FINDER	ASSIGNMENT	DUE
FRIDAY			
MATH			
SCIENCE			
HISTORY/ SOC. STUDIES			
ENGLISH/ LANG. ARTS			
LONG TERM ASSIGNMENT	PLANNING STRATEGIC TIP	NEXT	
OTHER THINGS TO REMEMBER		X _____	

FIVE DAY FORECAST

	MONDAY	TUESDAY	WEDNESDAY	THURSDAY	FRIDAY
BEFORE SCHOOL					
DURING SCHOOL					
AFTER SCHOOL					
EVENING					
BEFORE BED Homework	READY TO GO	READY TO GO	READY TO GO	READY TO GO	READY TO GO

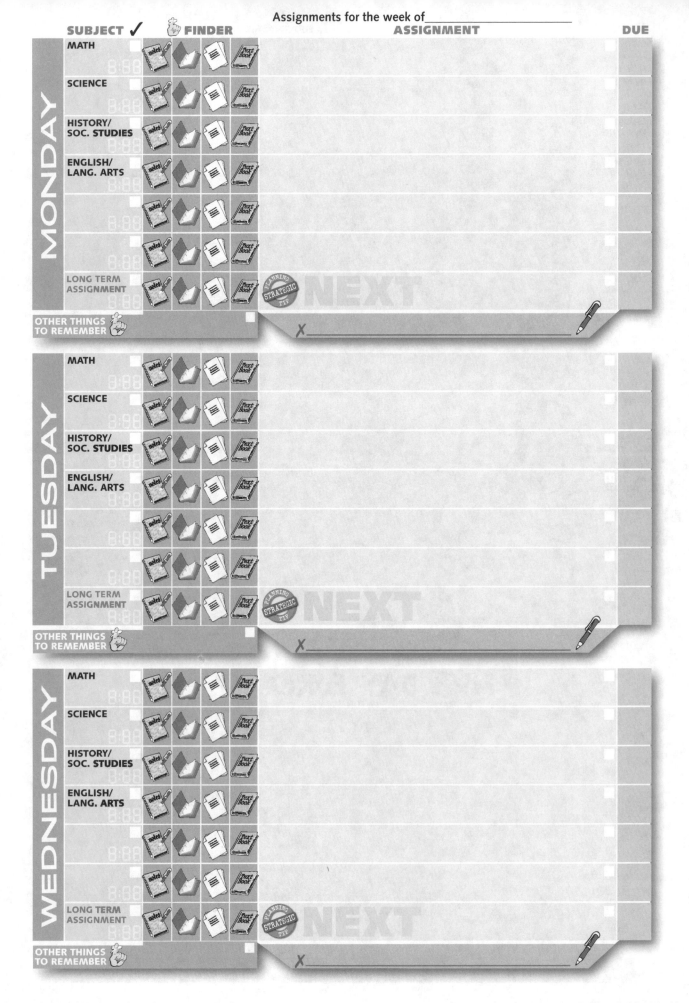

Assignments for the week of_____

SUBJECT ✓ FINDER ASSIGNMENT DUE

MONDAY

| MATH |
| SCIENCE |
| HISTORY/ SOC. STUDIES |
| ENGLISH/ LANG. ARTS |
| LONG TERM ASSIGNMENT |

OTHER THINGS TO REMEMBER

STRATEGIC PLANNING TIP — NEXT

X_____

TUESDAY

| MATH |
| SCIENCE |
| HISTORY/ SOC. STUDIES |
| ENGLISH/ LANG. ARTS |
| LONG TERM ASSIGNMENT |

OTHER THINGS TO REMEMBER

STRATEGIC PLANNING TIP — NEXT

X_____

WEDNESDAY

| MATH |
| SCIENCE |
| HISTORY/ SOC. STUDIES |
| ENGLISH/ LANG. ARTS |
| LONG TERM ASSIGNMENT |

OTHER THINGS TO REMEMBER

STRATEGIC PLANNING TIP — NEXT

X_____

SUBJECT ✓	FINDER	ASSIGNMENT	DUE

THURSDAY

- MATH
- SCIENCE
- HISTORY/ SOC. STUDIES
- ENGLISH/ LANG. ARTS
- LONG TERM ASSIGNMENT

NEXT

OTHER THINGS TO REMEMBER

X _____

FRIDAY

- MATH
- SCIENCE
- HISTORY/ SOC. STUDIES
- ENGLISH/ LANG. ARTS
- LONG TERM ASSIGNMENT

NEXT

OTHER THINGS TO REMEMBER

X _____

FIVE DAY FORECAST

	MONDAY	TUESDAY	WEDNESDAY	THURSDAY	FRIDAY
BEFORE SCHOOL					
DURING SCHOOL					
AFTER SCHOOL					
EVENING					
BEFORE BED					
Homework	READY TO GO	READY TO GO	READY TO GO	READY TO GO	READY TO GO

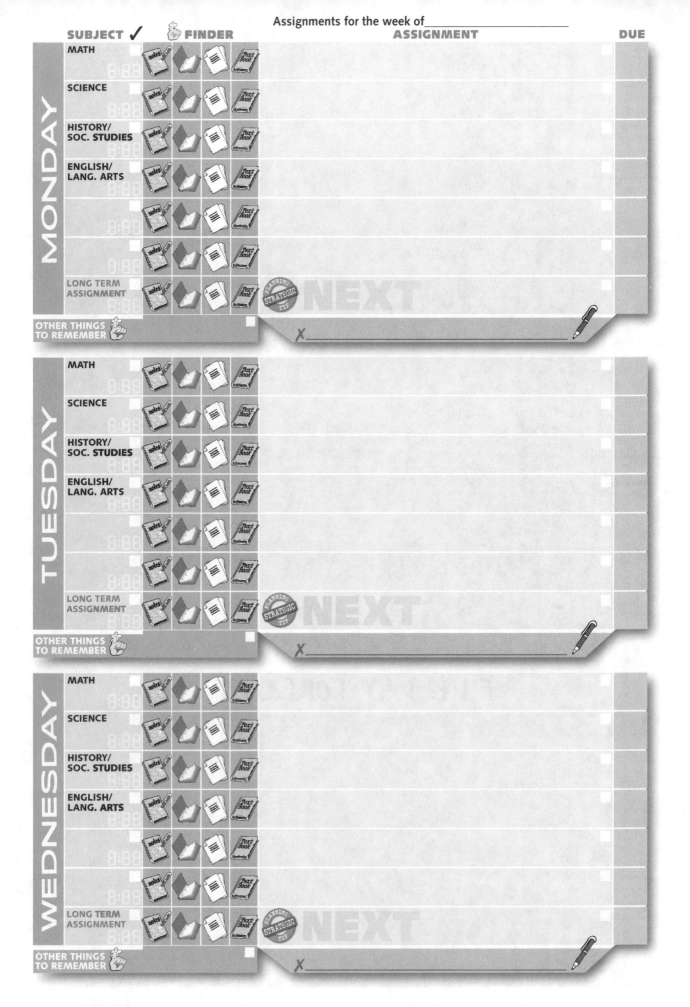

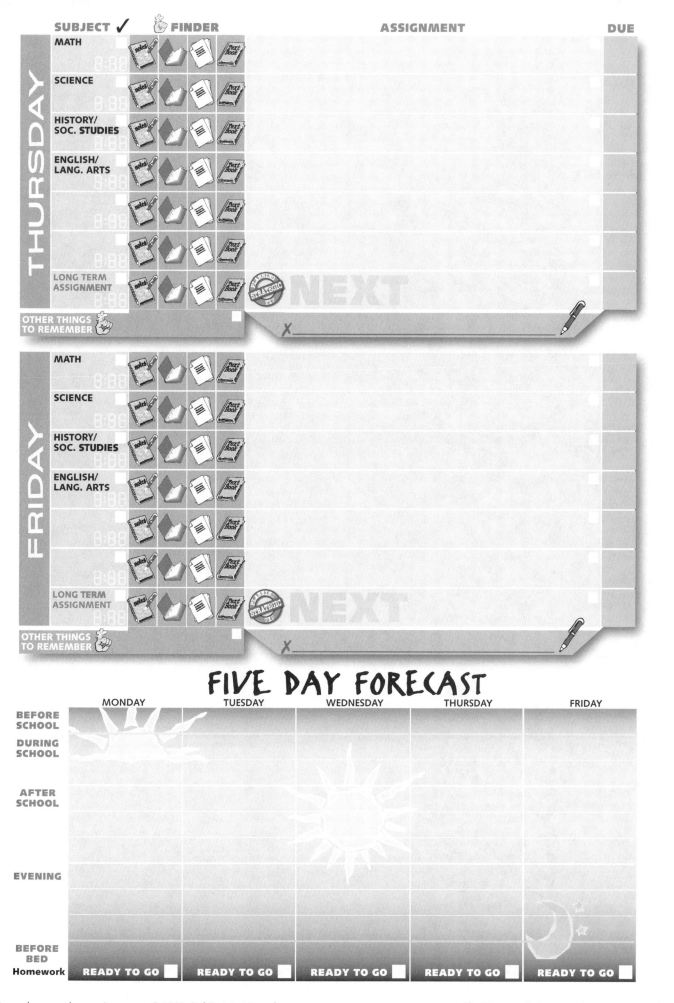

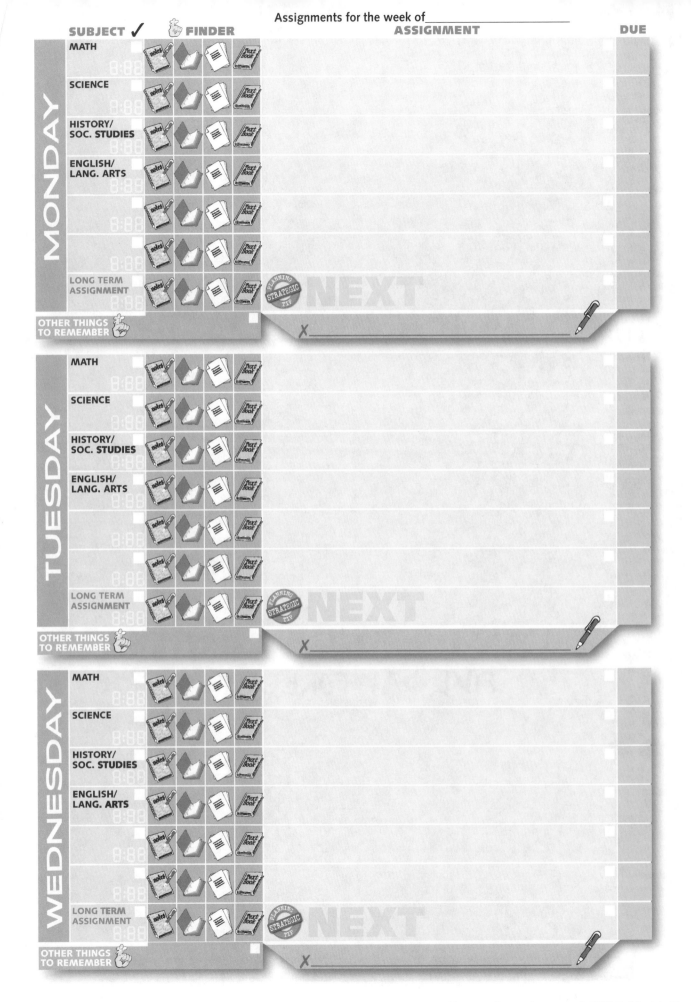

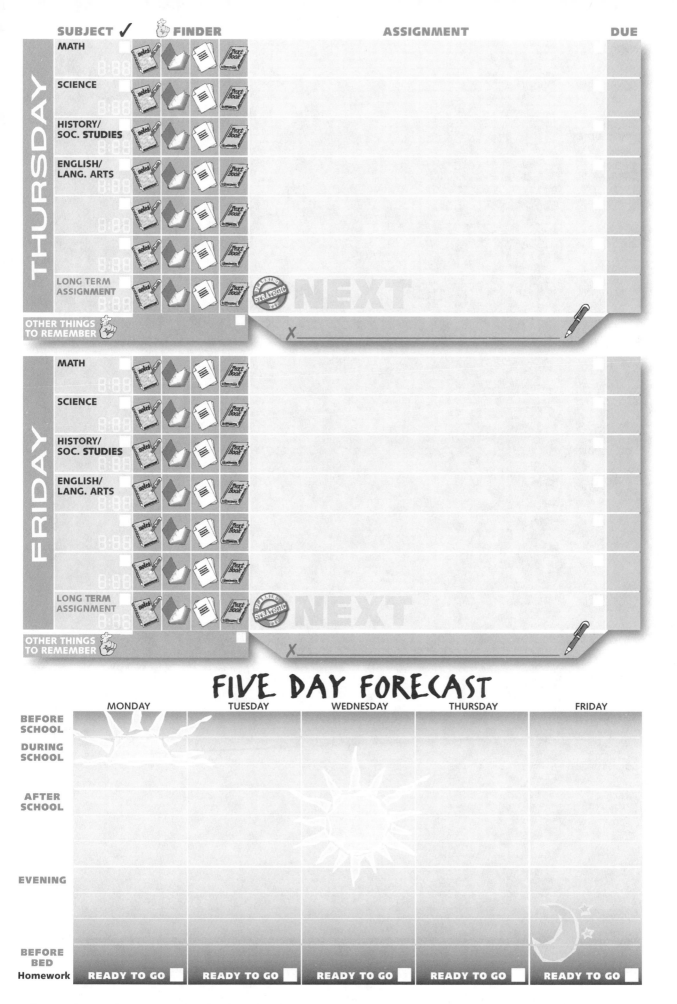

SUBJECT ✓	FINDER	ASSIGNMENT	DUE

THURSDAY

MATH			
SCIENCE			
HISTORY/ SOC. STUDIES			
ENGLISH/ LANG. ARTS			
LONG TERM ASSIGNMENT		NEXT	

OTHER THINGS TO REMEMBER

X _____

FRIDAY

MATH			
SCIENCE			
HISTORY/ SOC. STUDIES			
ENGLISH/ LANG. ARTS			
LONG TERM ASSIGNMENT		NEXT	

OTHER THINGS TO REMEMBER

X _____

FIVE DAY FORECAST

	MONDAY	TUESDAY	WEDNESDAY	THURSDAY	FRIDAY
BEFORE SCHOOL					
DURING SCHOOL					
AFTER SCHOOL					
EVENING					
BEFORE BED **Homework**	READY TO GO	READY TO GO	READY TO GO	READY TO GO	READY TO GO

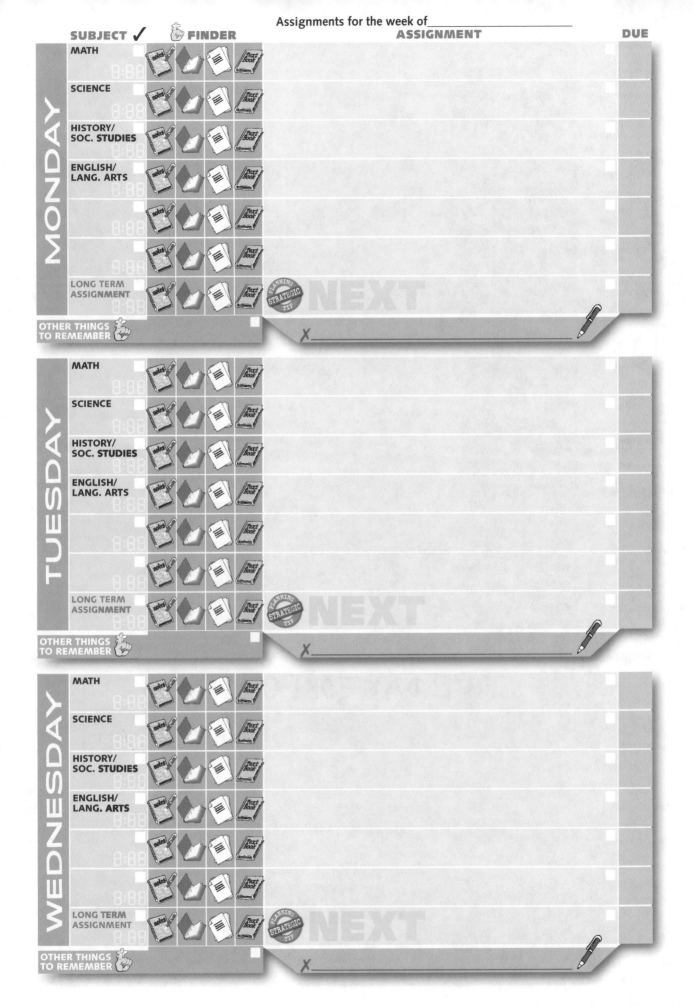

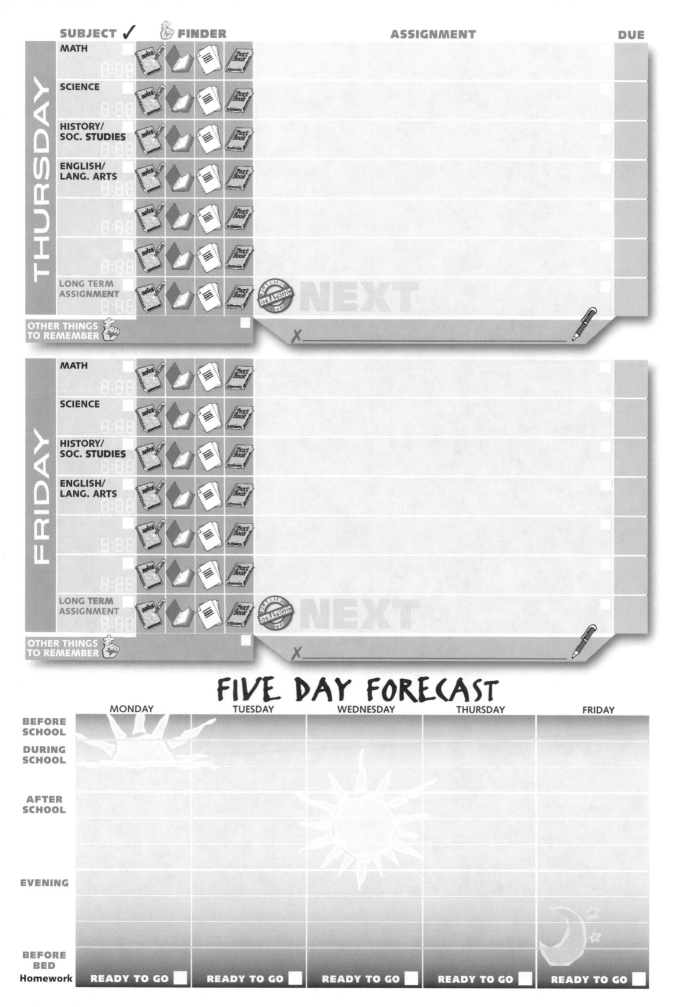

FIVE DAY FORECAST

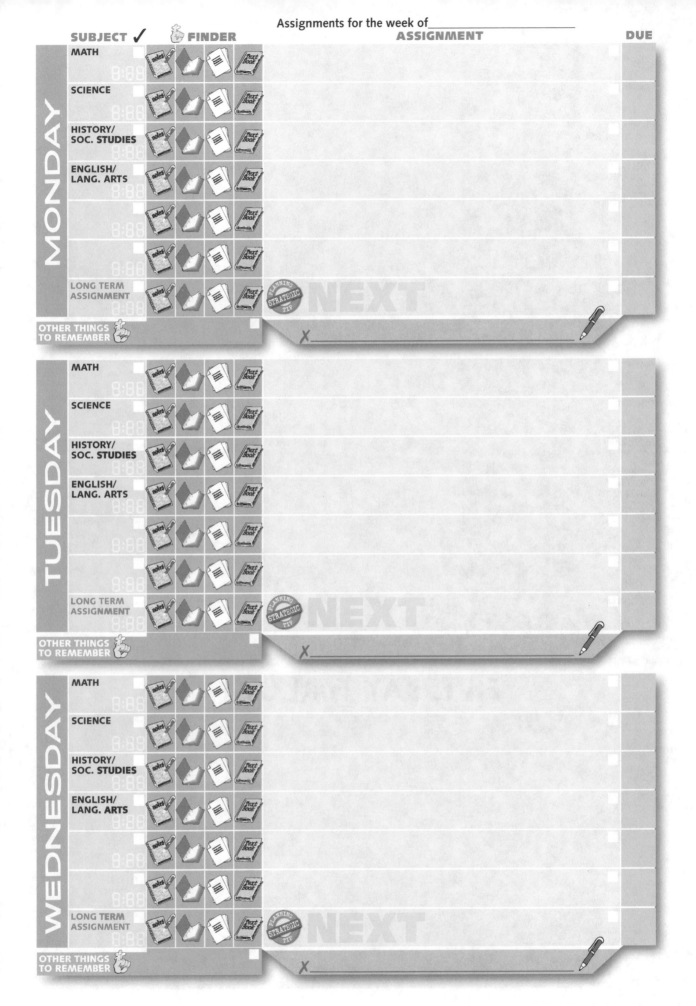

Assignments for the week of_____

SUBJECT ✓   FINDER   ASSIGNMENT   DUE

MONDAY
- MATH
- SCIENCE
- HISTORY/ SOC. STUDIES
- ENGLISH/ LANG. ARTS
- LONG TERM ASSIGNMENT

OTHER THINGS TO REMEMBER

TUESDAY
- MATH
- SCIENCE
- HISTORY/ SOC. STUDIES
- ENGLISH/ LANG. ARTS
- LONG TERM ASSIGNMENT

OTHER THINGS TO REMEMBER

WEDNESDAY
- MATH
- SCIENCE
- HISTORY/ SOC. STUDIES
- ENGLISH/ LANG. ARTS
- LONG TERM ASSIGNMENT

OTHER THINGS TO REMEMBER

PLANNING STRATEGIC TIP — NEXT

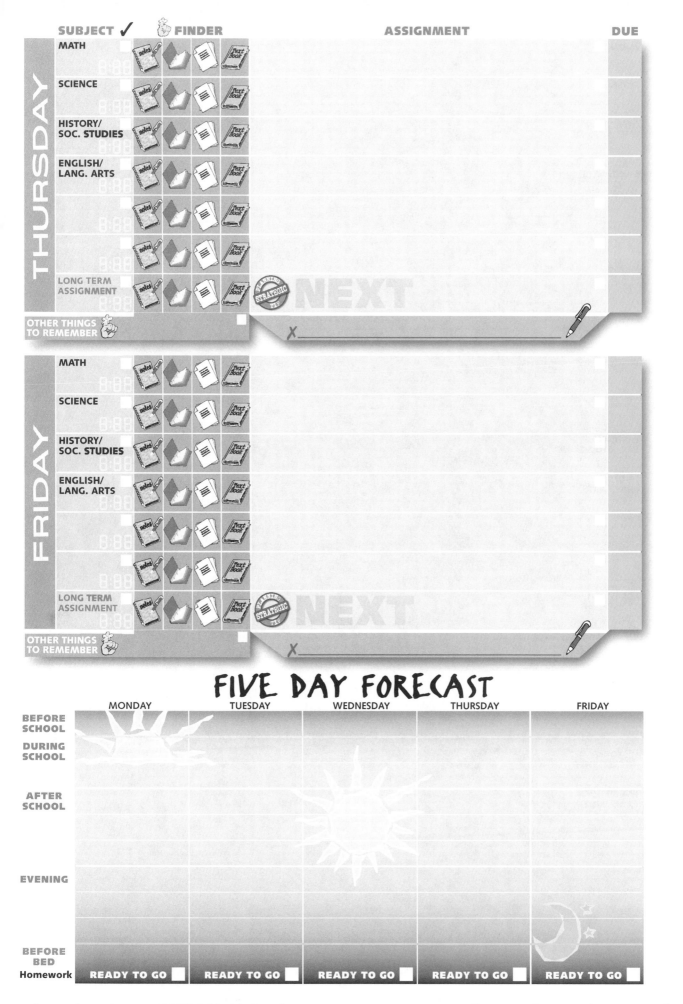

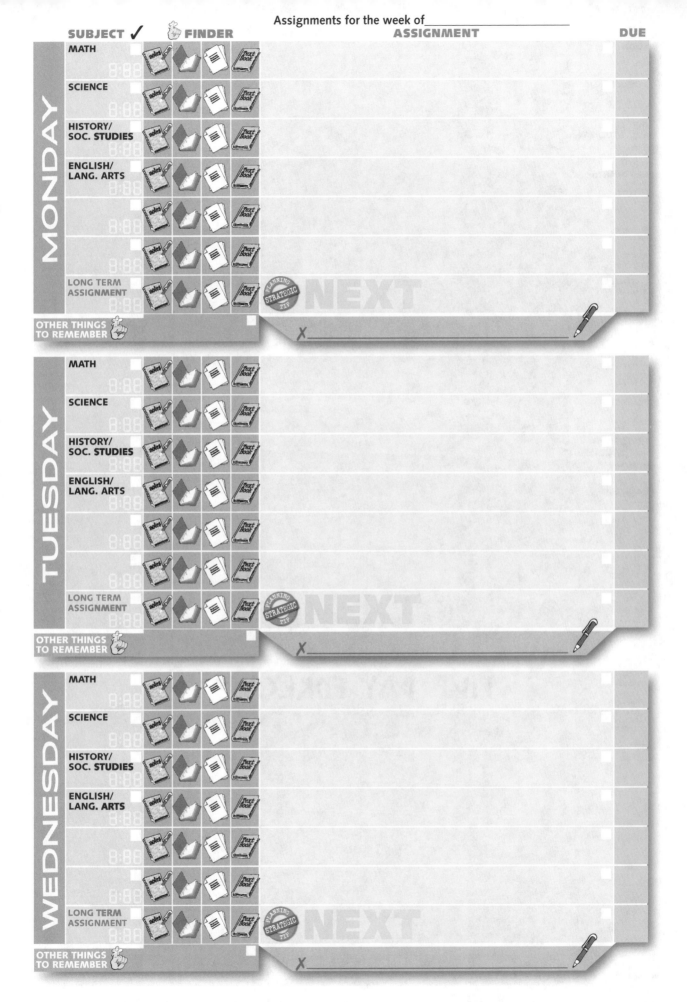

The Homework Organizer by Get Organized!

www.homework-organizer.com • © 2002 Gail Epstein Mengel

SUBJECT ✓	🖐 FINDER	ASSIGNMENT	DUE
THURSDAY			
MATH			
SCIENCE			
HISTORY/ SOC. STUDIES			
ENGLISH/ LANG. ARTS			
LONG TERM ASSIGNMENT		NEXT	
OTHER THINGS TO REMEMBER 🖐		X _____	

FRIDAY			
MATH			
SCIENCE			
HISTORY/ SOC. STUDIES			
ENGLISH/ LANG. ARTS			
LONG TERM ASSIGNMENT		NEXT	
OTHER THINGS TO REMEMBER 🖐		X _____	

FIVE DAY FORECAST

	MONDAY	TUESDAY	WEDNESDAY	THURSDAY	FRIDAY
BEFORE SCHOOL					
DURING SCHOOL					
AFTER SCHOOL					
EVENING					
BEFORE BED					
Homework	READY TO GO ☐	READY TO GO ☐	READY TO GO ☐	READY TO GO ☐	READY TO GO ☐

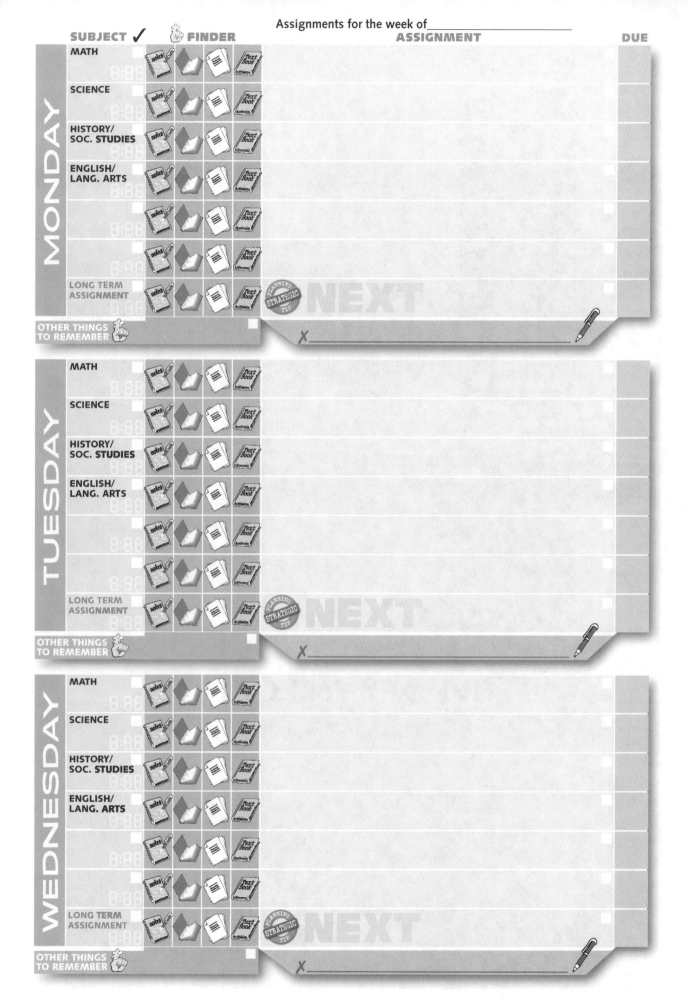

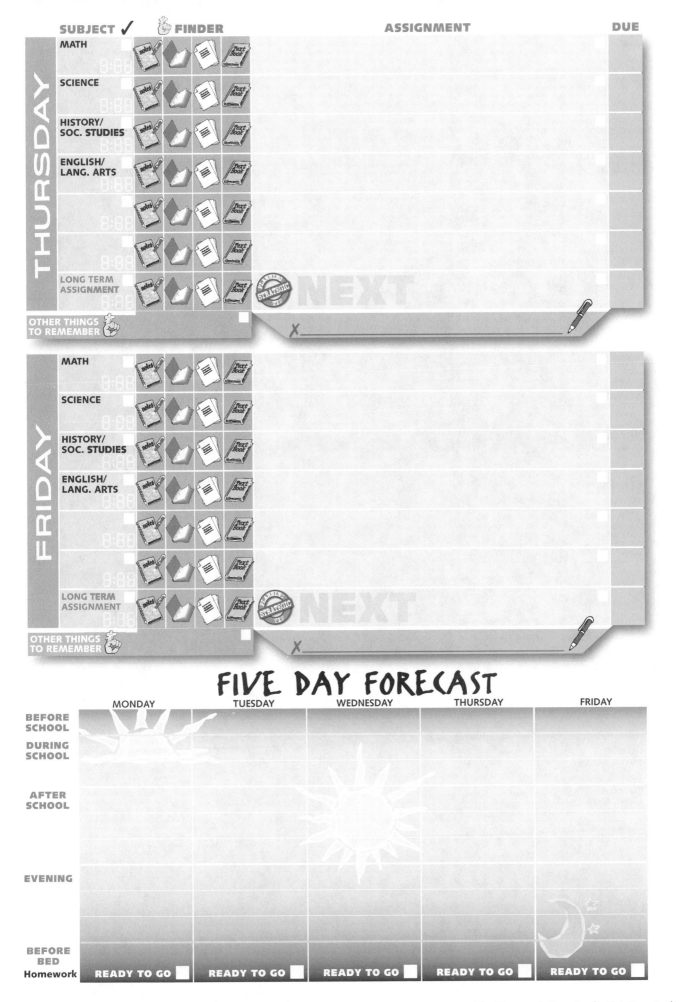

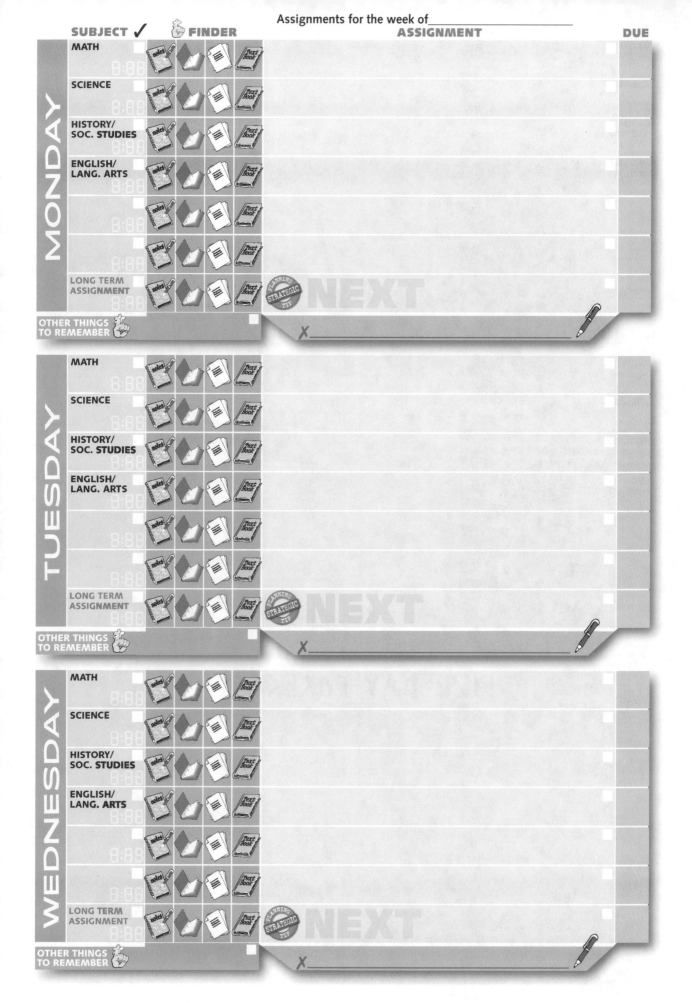

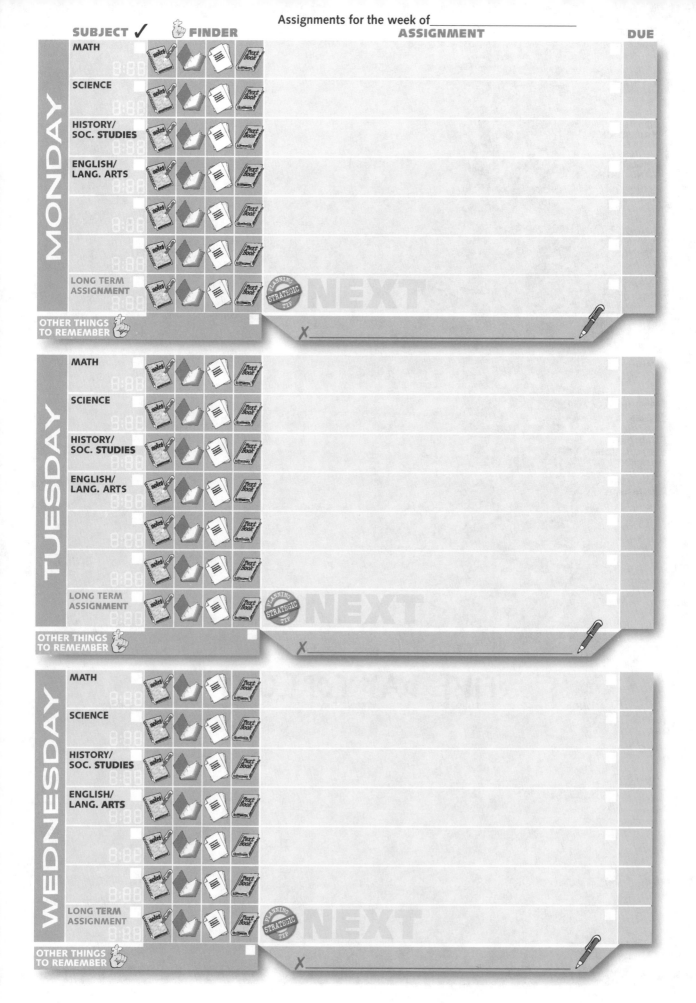

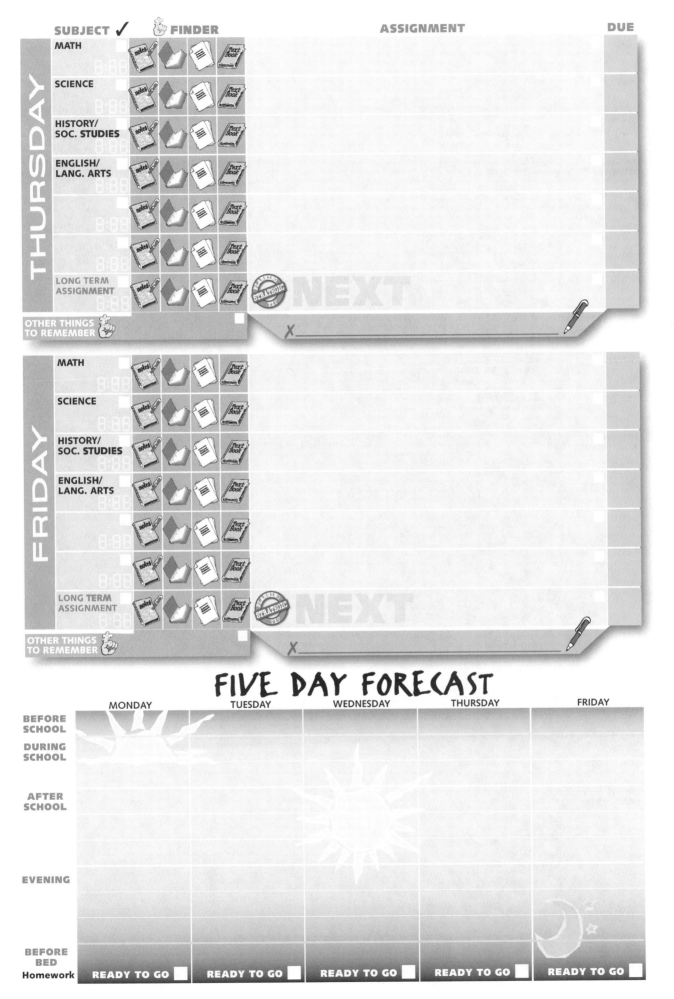

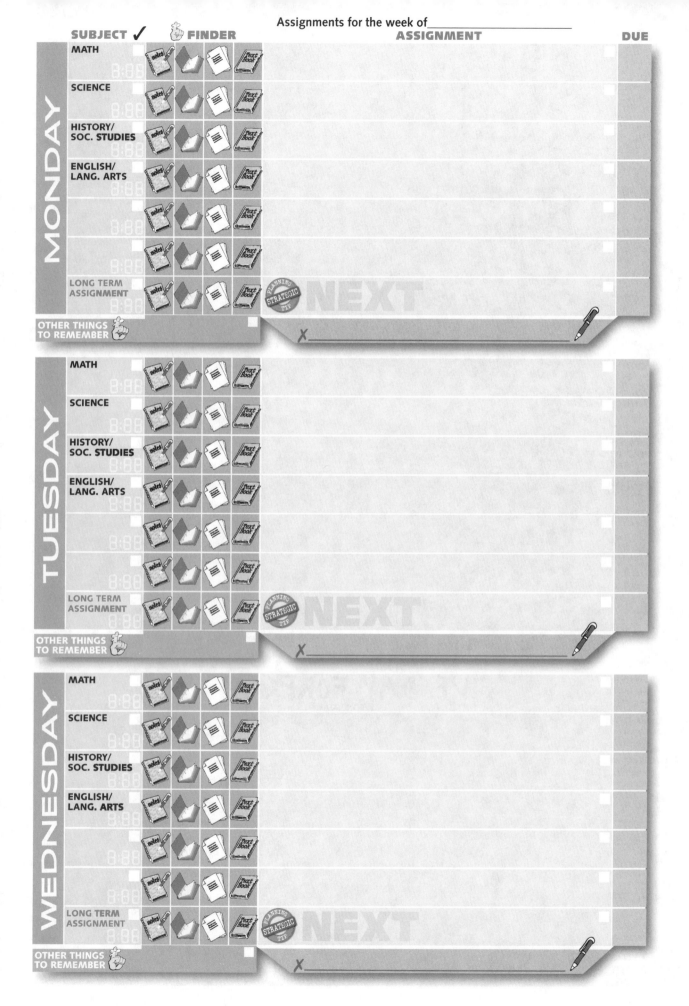

Assignments for the week of _____

SUBJECT ✓   **FINDER**   **ASSIGNMENT**   **DUE**

MONDAY
- MATH
- SCIENCE
- HISTORY/ SOC. STUDIES
- ENGLISH/ LANG. ARTS
- LONG TERM ASSIGNMENT

OTHER THINGS TO REMEMBER

TUESDAY
- MATH
- SCIENCE
- HISTORY/ SOC. STUDIES
- ENGLISH/ LANG. ARTS
- LONG TERM ASSIGNMENT

OTHER THINGS TO REMEMBER

WEDNESDAY
- MATH
- SCIENCE
- HISTORY/ SOC. STUDIES
- ENGLISH/ LANG. ARTS
- LONG TERM ASSIGNMENT

OTHER THINGS TO REMEMBER

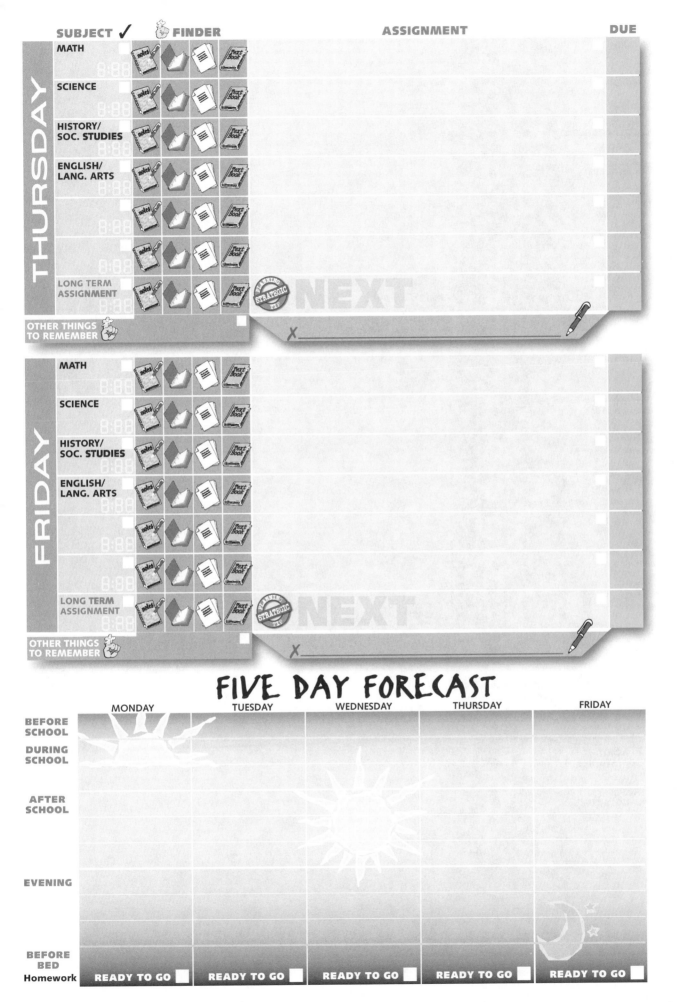

SUBJECT ✓	FINDER	ASSIGNMENT	DUE
MATH 8:88			
SCIENCE 8:88			
HISTORY/ SOC. STUDIES 8:88			
ENGLISH/ LANG. ARTS 8:88			
8:88			
8:88			
LONG TERM ASSIGNMENT 8:88		STRATEGIC NEXT	

THURSDAY

OTHER THINGS TO REMEMBER X _____

SUBJECT ✓	FINDER	ASSIGNMENT	DUE
MATH 8:88			
SCIENCE 8:88			
HISTORY/ SOC. STUDIES 8:88			
ENGLISH/ LANG. ARTS 8:88			
8:88			
8:88			
LONG TERM ASSIGNMENT 8:88		STRATEGIC NEXT	

FRIDAY

OTHER THINGS TO REMEMBER X _____

FIVE DAY FORECAST

	MONDAY	TUESDAY	WEDNESDAY	THURSDAY	FRIDAY
BEFORE SCHOOL					
DURING SCHOOL					
AFTER SCHOOL					
EVENING					
BEFORE BED **Homework**	READY TO GO	READY TO GO	READY TO GO	READY TO GO	READY TO GO

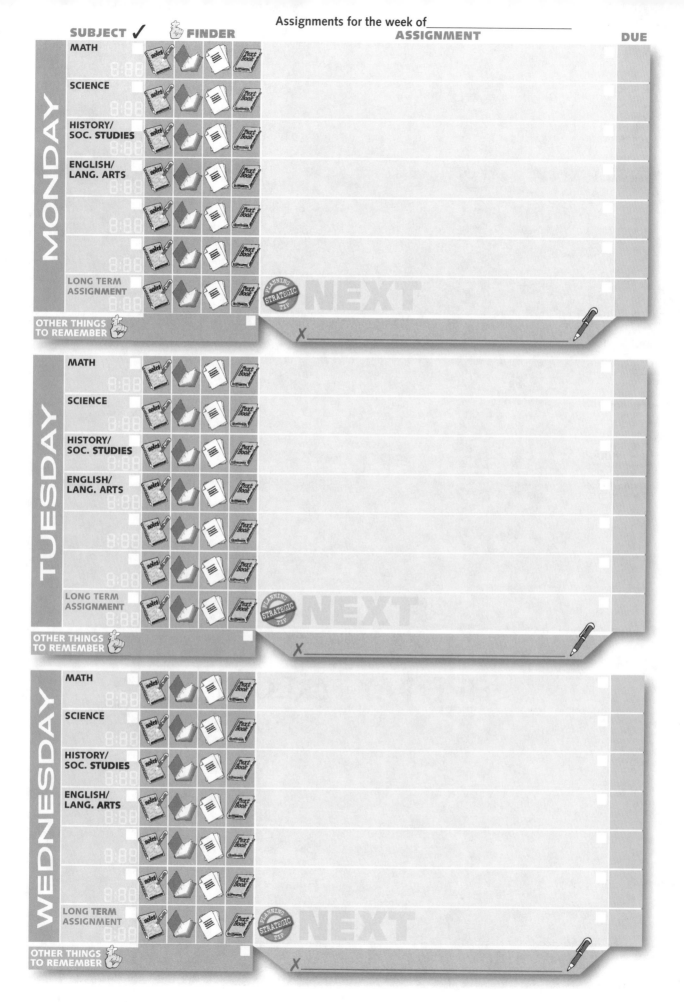

SUBJECT ✓	FINDER	ASSIGNMENT	DUE
THURSDAY			
MATH			
SCIENCE			
HISTORY/ SOC. STUDIES			
ENGLISH/ LANG. ARTS			
LONG TERM ASSIGNMENT		NEXT	
OTHER THINGS TO REMEMBER		X_____	

SUBJECT ✓	FINDER	ASSIGNMENT	DUE
FRIDAY			
MATH			
SCIENCE			
HISTORY/ SOC. STUDIES			
ENGLISH/ LANG. ARTS			
LONG TERM ASSIGNMENT		NEXT	
OTHER THINGS TO REMEMBER		X_____	

FIVE DAY FORECAST

	MONDAY	TUESDAY	WEDNESDAY	THURSDAY	FRIDAY
BEFORE SCHOOL					
DURING SCHOOL					
AFTER SCHOOL					
EVENING					
BEFORE BED					
Homework	READY TO GO	READY TO GO	READY TO GO	READY TO GO	READY TO GO

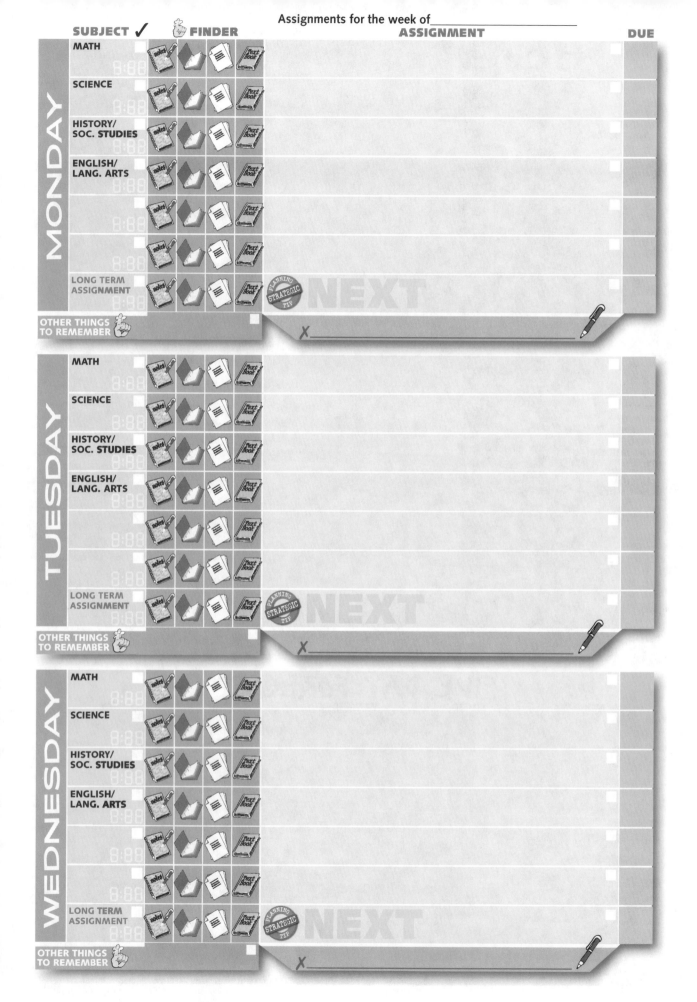

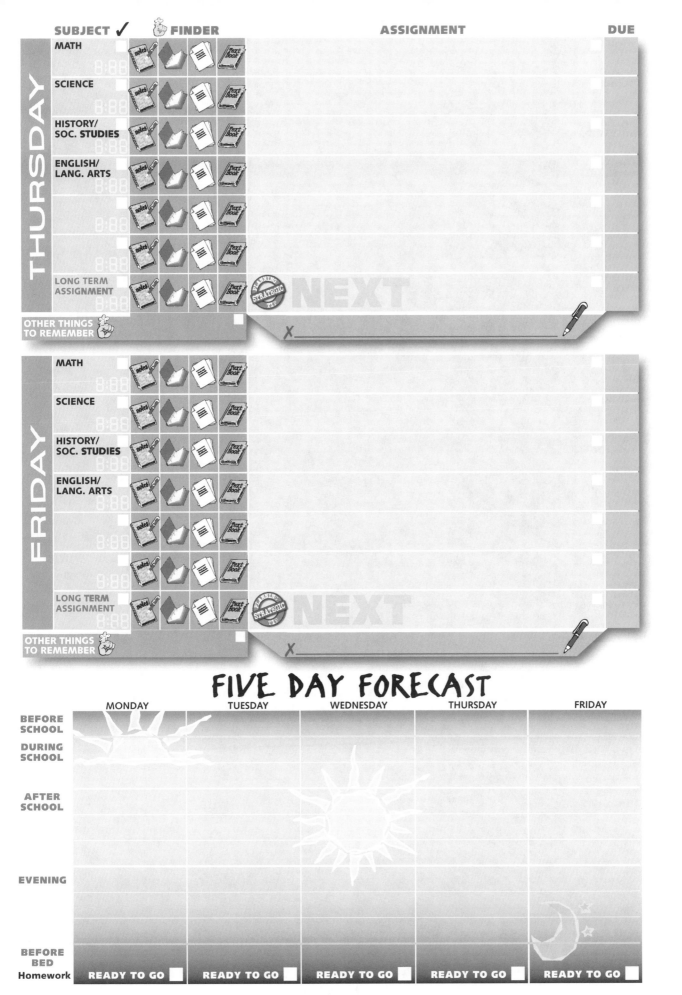

SUBJECT ✓	FINDER	ASSIGNMENT	DUE

THURSDAY

- MATH
- SCIENCE
- HISTORY/ SOC. STUDIES
- ENGLISH/ LANG. ARTS
- LONG TERM ASSIGNMENT

OTHER THINGS TO REMEMBER

NEXT X _____

FRIDAY

- MATH
- SCIENCE
- HISTORY/ SOC. STUDIES
- ENGLISH/ LANG. ARTS
- LONG TERM ASSIGNMENT

OTHER THINGS TO REMEMBER

NEXT X _____

FIVE DAY FORECAST

	MONDAY	TUESDAY	WEDNESDAY	THURSDAY	FRIDAY
BEFORE SCHOOL					
DURING SCHOOL					
AFTER SCHOOL					
EVENING					
BEFORE BED Homework	READY TO GO	READY TO GO	READY TO GO	READY TO GO	READY TO GO

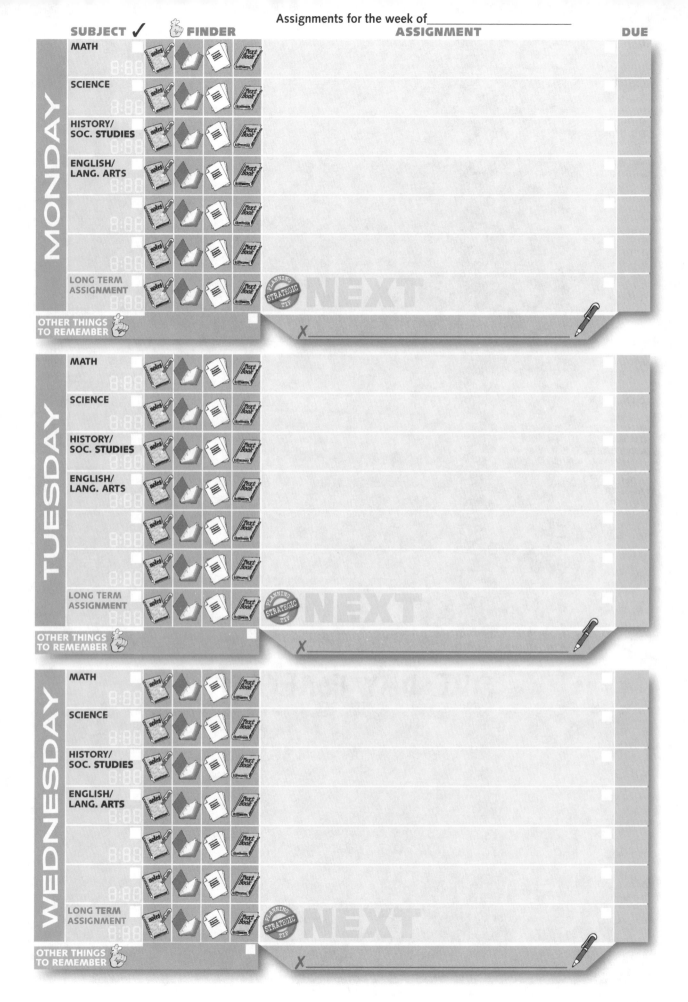

Assignments for the week of _____

SUBJECT ✓   **FINDER**   **ASSIGNMENT**   **DUE**

MONDAY
- MATH
- SCIENCE
- HISTORY/ SOC. STUDIES
- ENGLISH/ LANG. ARTS
- LONG TERM ASSIGNMENT

OTHER THINGS TO REMEMBER

TUESDAY
- MATH
- SCIENCE
- HISTORY/ SOC. STUDIES
- ENGLISH/ LANG. ARTS
- LONG TERM ASSIGNMENT

OTHER THINGS TO REMEMBER

WEDNESDAY
- MATH
- SCIENCE
- HISTORY/ SOC. STUDIES
- ENGLISH/ LANG. ARTS
- LONG TERM ASSIGNMENT

OTHER THINGS TO REMEMBER

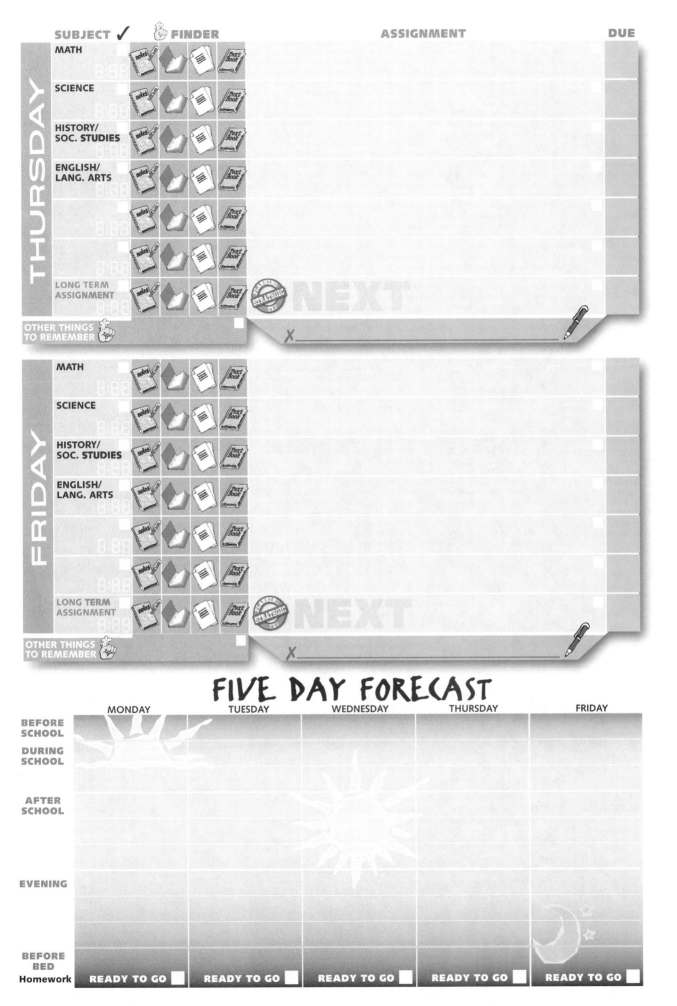

SUBJECT ✓	FINDER				ASSIGNMENT	DUE
THURSDAY						
MATH						
SCIENCE						
HISTORY/ SOC. STUDIES						
ENGLISH/ LANG. ARTS						
LONG TERM ASSIGNMENT					*STRATEGIC* NEXT	
OTHER THINGS TO REMEMBER					X _____	

SUBJECT ✓	FINDER				ASSIGNMENT	DUE
FRIDAY						
MATH						
SCIENCE						
HISTORY/ SOC. STUDIES						
ENGLISH/ LANG. ARTS						
LONG TERM ASSIGNMENT					*STRATEGIC* NEXT	
OTHER THINGS TO REMEMBER					X _____	

FIVE DAY FORECAST

	MONDAY	TUESDAY	WEDNESDAY	THURSDAY	FRIDAY
BEFORE SCHOOL					
DURING SCHOOL					
AFTER SCHOOL					
EVENING					
BEFORE BED					
Homework	READY TO GO ☐	READY TO GO ☐	READY TO GO ☐	READY TO GO ☐	READY TO GO ☐

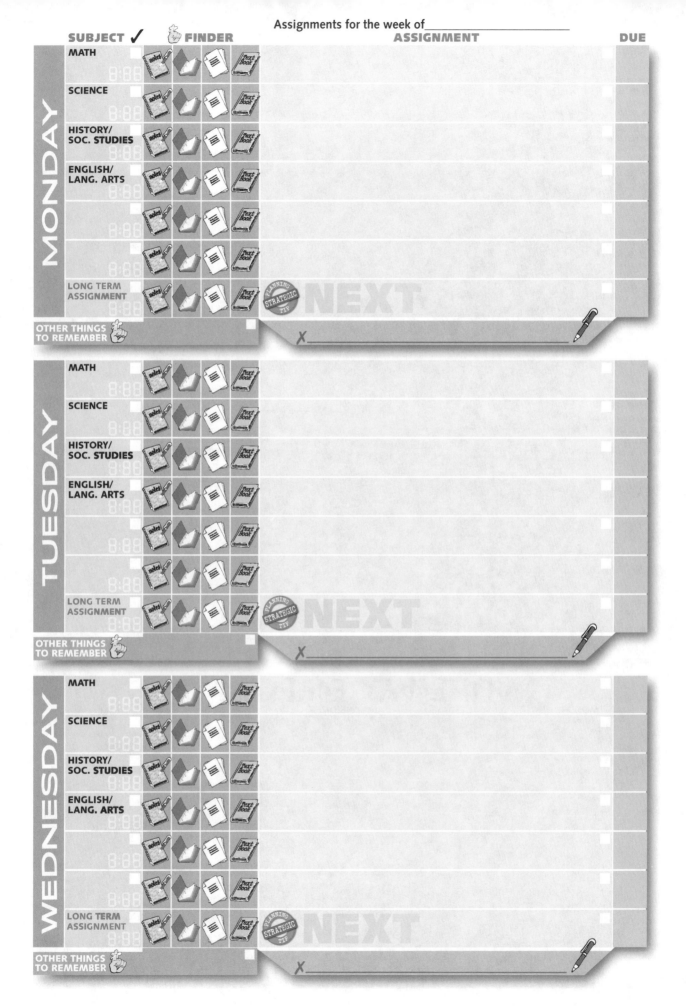

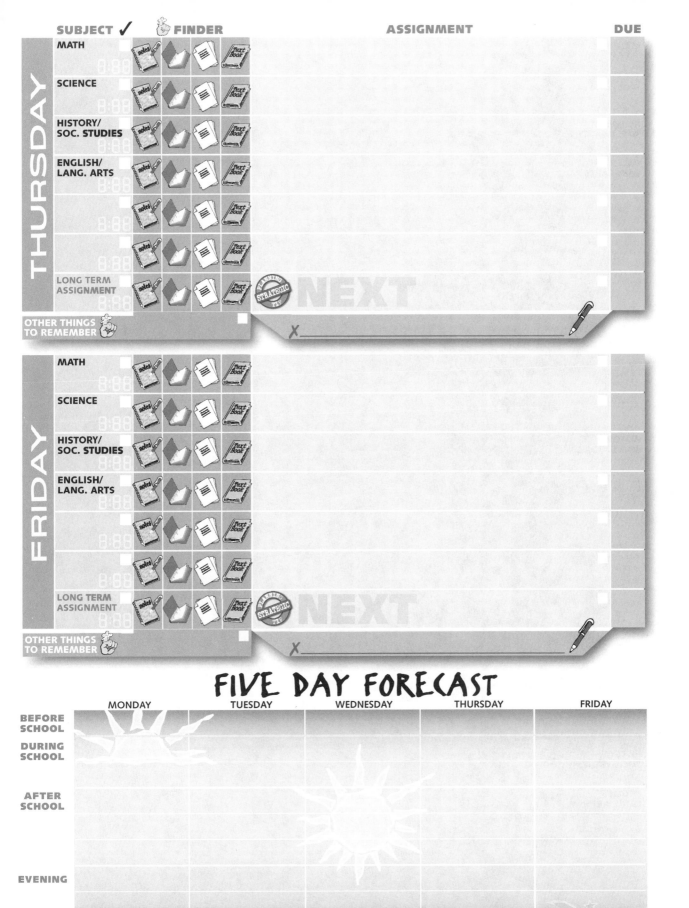

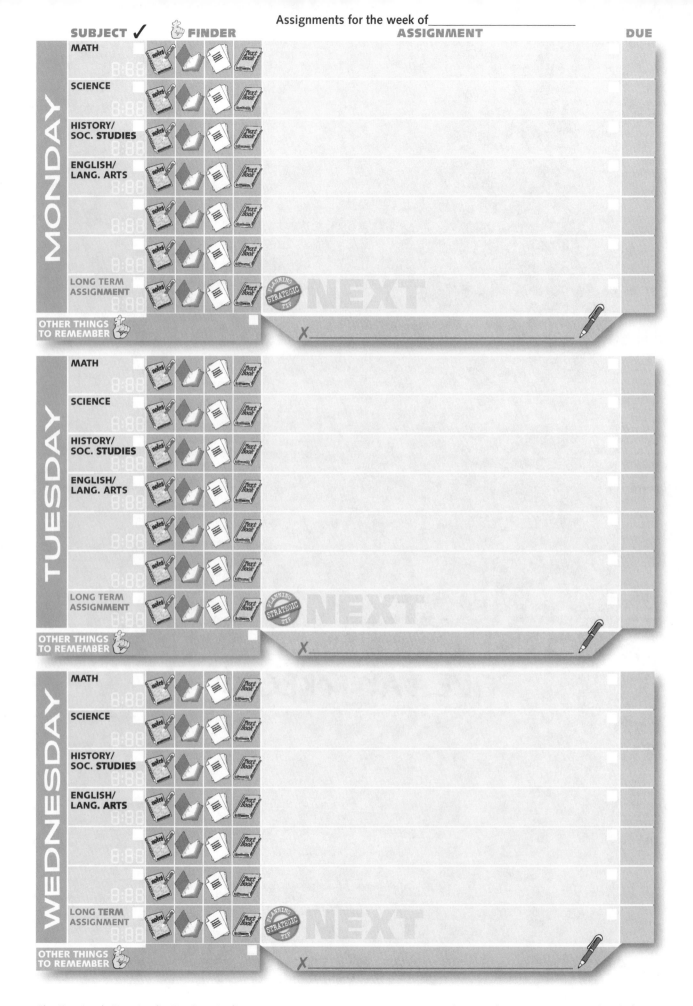

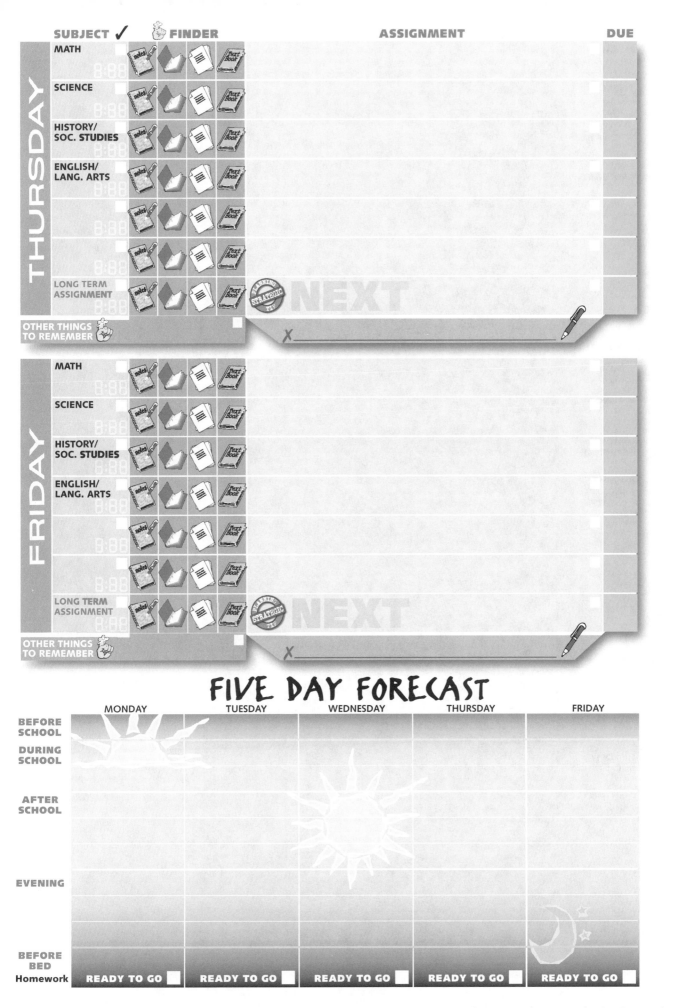

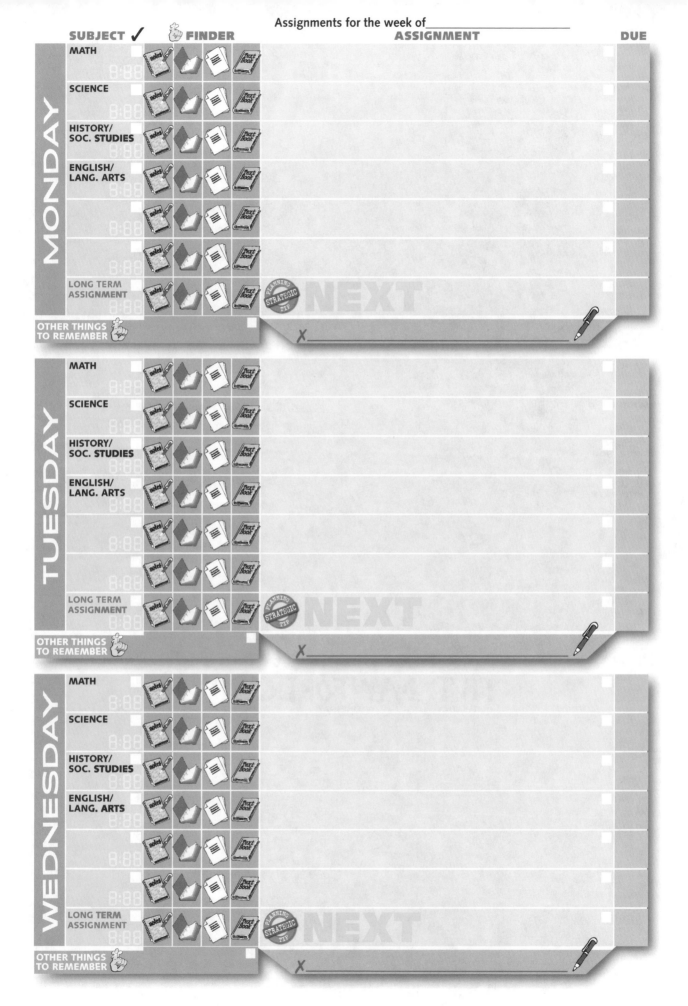

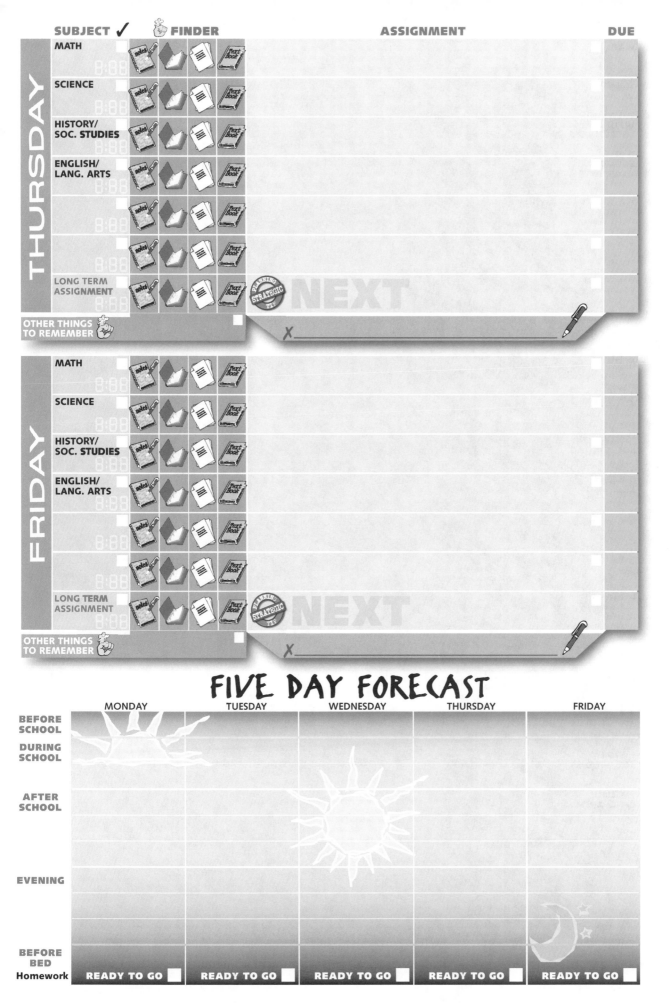

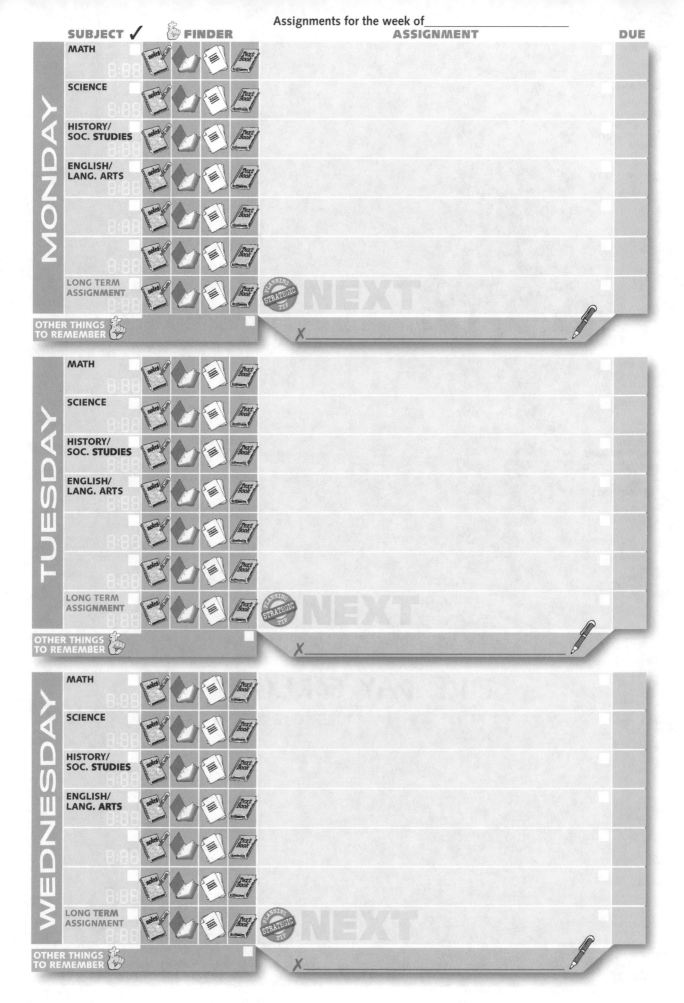

Assignments for the week of_____

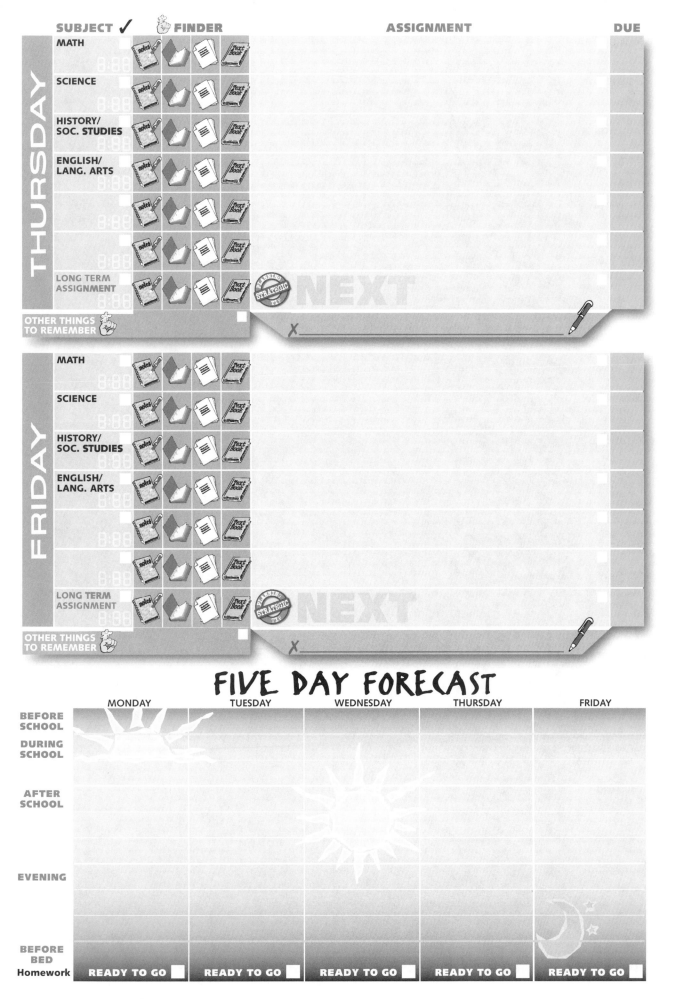

SUBJECT ✓	FINDER				ASSIGNMENT	DUE
THURSDAY MATH	notes			Text Book		
SCIENCE	notes			Text Book		
HISTORY/ SOC. STUDIES	notes			Text Book		
ENGLISH/ LANG. ARTS	notes			Text Book		
	notes			Text Book		
	notes			Text Book		
LONG TERM ASSIGNMENT	notes			Text Book	STRATEGIC NEXT	
OTHER THINGS TO REMEMBER					X _____	

SUBJECT	FINDER				ASSIGNMENT	DUE
FRIDAY MATH	notes			Text Book		
SCIENCE	notes			Text Book		
HISTORY/ SOC. STUDIES	notes			Text Book		
ENGLISH/ LANG. ARTS	notes			Text Book		
	notes			Text Book		
	notes			Text Book		
LONG TERM ASSIGNMENT	notes			Text Book	STRATEGIC NEXT	
OTHER THINGS TO REMEMBER					X _____	

FIVE DAY FORECAST

	MONDAY	TUESDAY	WEDNESDAY	THURSDAY	FRIDAY
BEFORE SCHOOL					
DURING SCHOOL					
AFTER SCHOOL					
EVENING					
BEFORE BED					
Homework	READY TO GO	READY TO GO	READY TO GO	READY TO GO	READY TO GO

Assignments for the week of_____

SUBJECT ✓	FINDER	ASSIGNMENT	DUE

MONDAY

MATH			
SCIENCE			
HISTORY/ SOC. STUDIES			
ENGLISH/ LANG. ARTS			
LONG TERM ASSIGNMENT		STRATEGIC PLANNING TIP	NEXT

OTHER THINGS TO REMEMBER
X_____

TUESDAY

MATH			
SCIENCE			
HISTORY/ SOC. STUDIES			
ENGLISH/ LANG. ARTS			
LONG TERM ASSIGNMENT		STRATEGIC PLANNING TIP	NEXT

OTHER THINGS TO REMEMBER
X_____

WEDNESDAY

MATH			
SCIENCE			
HISTORY/ SOC. STUDIES			
ENGLISH/ LANG. ARTS			
LONG TERM ASSIGNMENT		STRATEGIC PLANNING TIP	NEXT

OTHER THINGS TO REMEMBER
X_____

SUBJECT ✓	🐭 FINDER	ASSIGNMENT	DUE

THURSDAY

MATH			
SCIENCE			
HISTORY/ SOC. STUDIES			
ENGLISH/ LANG. ARTS			
LONG TERM ASSIGNMENT		**NEXT**	

OTHER THINGS TO REMEMBER

X _____

FRIDAY

MATH			
SCIENCE			
HISTORY/ SOC. STUDIES			
ENGLISH/ LANG. ARTS			
LONG TERM ASSIGNMENT		**NEXT**	

OTHER THINGS TO REMEMBER

X _____

FIVE DAY FORECAST

	MONDAY	TUESDAY	WEDNESDAY	THURSDAY	FRIDAY
BEFORE SCHOOL					
DURING SCHOOL					
AFTER SCHOOL					
EVENING					
BEFORE BED					
Homework	READY TO GO	READY TO GO	READY TO GO	READY TO GO	READY TO GO

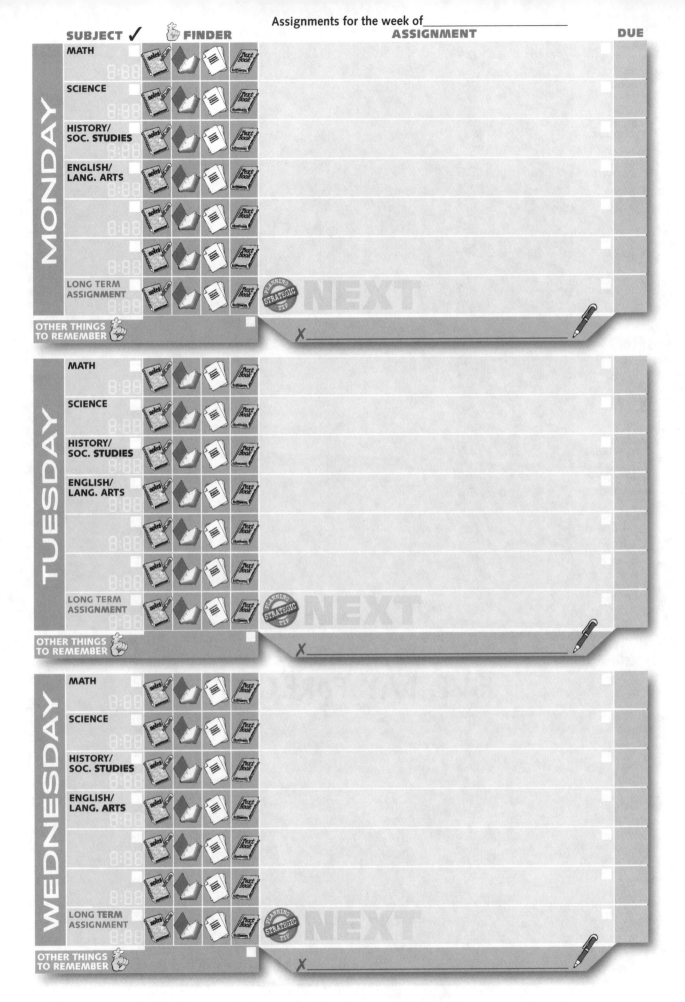

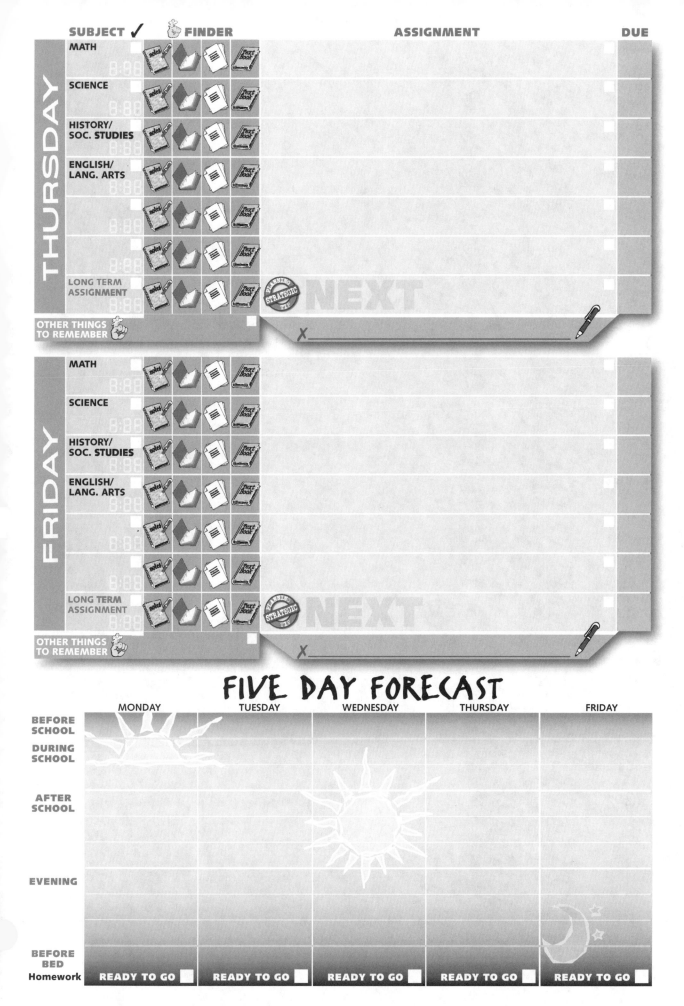

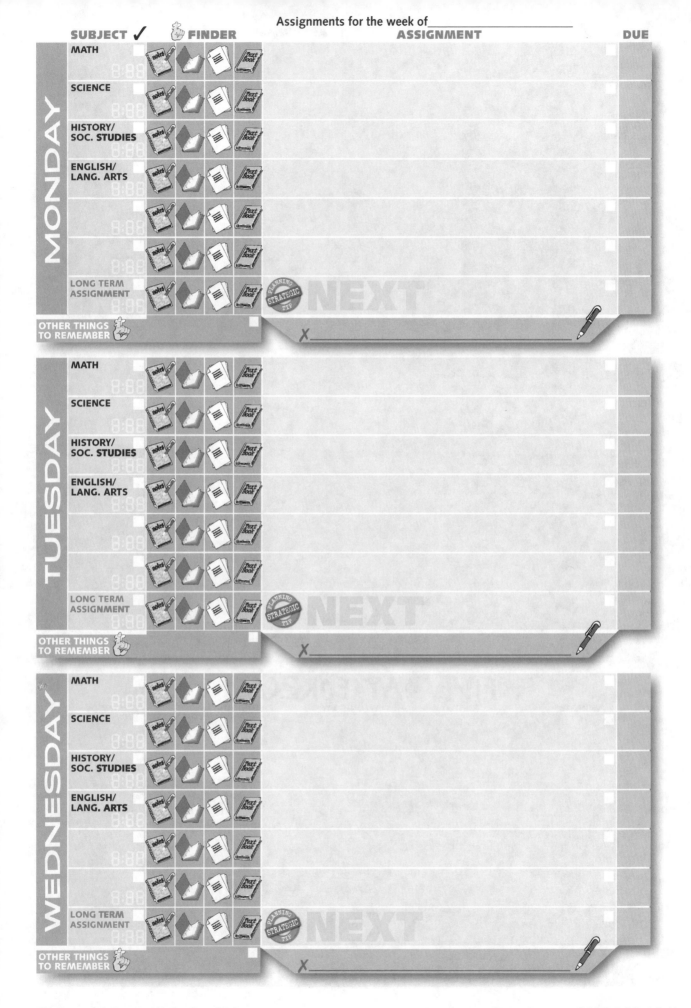

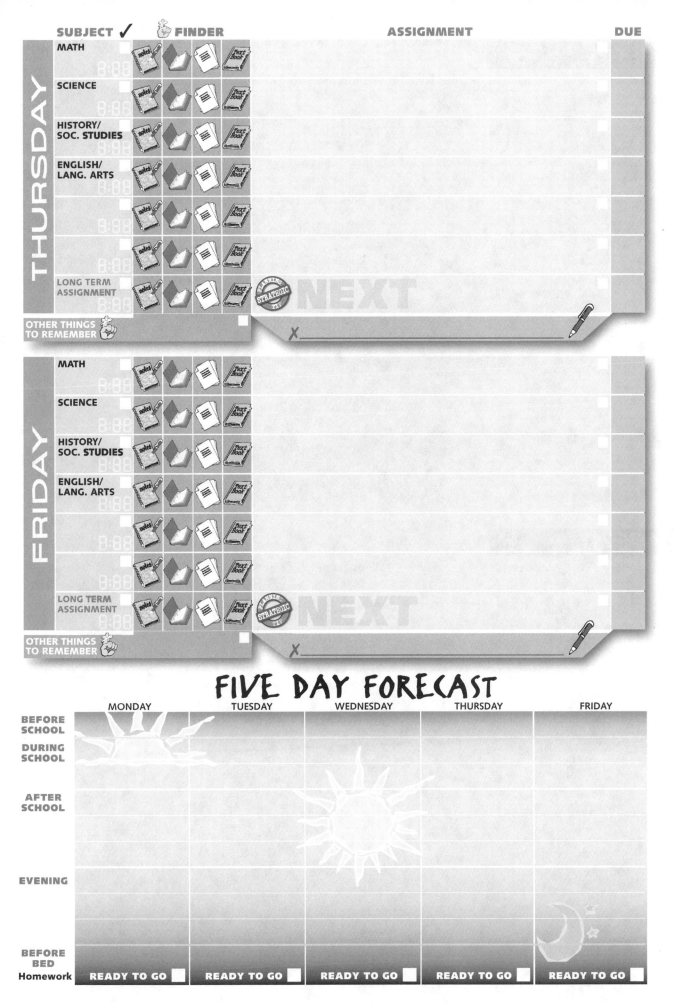

SUBJECT ✓	🐥 FINDER				ASSIGNMENT	DUE

THURSDAY

MATH						
8:88	notes			Text Book		
SCIENCE						
8:88	notes			Text Book		
HISTORY/ SOC. STUDIES						
8:88	notes			Text Book		
ENGLISH/ LANG. ARTS						
8:88	notes			Text Book		
	notes			Text Book		
8:88						
	notes			Text Book		
8:88						
LONG TERM ASSIGNMENT	notes			Text Book		
8:88						

PLANNING STRATEGIC TIP

NEXT

X_____

OTHER THINGS TO REMEMBER

FRIDAY

MATH						
8:88	notes			Text Book		
SCIENCE						
8:88	notes			Text Book		
HISTORY/ SOC. STUDIES						
8:88	notes			Text Book		
ENGLISH/ LANG. ARTS						
8:88	notes			Text Book		
	notes			Text Book		
8:88						
	notes			Text Book		
8:88						
LONG TERM ASSIGNMENT	notes			Text Book		
8:88						

PLANNING STRATEGIC TIP

NEXT

X_____

OTHER THINGS TO REMEMBER

FIVE DAY FORECAST

	MONDAY	TUESDAY	WEDNESDAY	THURSDAY	FRIDAY
BEFORE SCHOOL					
DURING SCHOOL					
AFTER SCHOOL					
EVENING					
BEFORE BED **Homework**	READY TO GO	READY TO GO	READY TO GO	READY TO GO	READY TO GO

Be careful: (1) Match the days and dates. (2) Write in the correct number of days for each month.

JULY

Sunday	Monday	Tuesday	Wednesday	Thursday	Friday	Saturday

AUGUST

Sunday	Monday	Tuesday	Wednesday	Thursday	Friday	Saturday

Be careful: (1) Match the days and dates. (2) Write in the correct number of days for each month.

SEPTEMBER

Sunday	Monday	Tuesday	Wednesday	Thursday	Friday	Saturday

OCTOBER

Sunday	Monday	Tuesday	Wednesday	Thursday	Friday	Saturday

Be careful: (1) Match the days and dates. (2) Write in the correct number of days for each month.

NOVEMBER

Sunday	Monday	Tuesday	Wednesday	Thursday	Friday	Saturday

DECEMBER

Sunday	Monday	Tuesday	Wednesday	Thursday	Friday	Saturday

Be careful: (1) Match the days and dates. (2) Write in the correct number of days for each month.

JANUARY

Sunday	Monday	Tuesday	Wednesday	Thursday	Friday	Saturday

FEBRUARY

Sunday	Monday	Tuesday	Wednesday	Thursday	Friday	Saturday

Be careful: (1) Match the days and dates. (2) Write in the correct number of days for each month.

MARCH

Sunday	Monday	Tuesday	Wednesday	Thursday	Friday	Saturday

APRIL

Sunday	Monday	Tuesday	Wednesday	Thursday	Friday	Saturday

Be careful: (1) Match the days and dates. (2) Write in the correct number of days for each month.

MAY

Sunday	Monday	Tuesday	Wednesday	Thursday	Friday	Saturday

JUNE

Sunday	Monday	Tuesday	Wednesday	Thursday	Friday	Saturday

TEACHER TRACKER 1

		MONDAY	TUESDAY	WEDNESDAY	THURSDAY	FRIDAY
SUBJECT	Time:					
TEACHER	Room:					
SUBJECT	Time:					
TEACHER	Room:					
SUBJECT	Time:					
TEACHER	Room:					
SUBJECT	Time:					
TEACHER	Room:					
SUBJECT	Time:					
TEACHER	Room:					
SUBJECT	Time:					
TEACHER	Room:					

DIRECTIONS: FIRST, ask your teachers the exact days, times, and places when they are available to help students. **THEN,** circle the times that best match your "free" time.

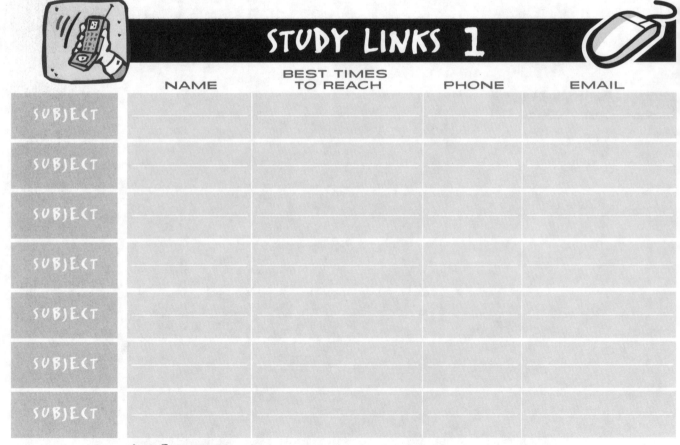

STUDY LINKS 1

	NAME	BEST TIMES TO REACH	PHONE	EMAIL
SUBJECT				
SUBJECT				
SUBJECT				
SUBJECT				
SUBJECT				
SUBJECT				
SUBJECT				

DIRECTIONS: In each subject, find two classmates you can depend on for help if you get stuck. Then fill in the information above.

TEACHER TRACKER 2

		MONDAY	TUESDAY	WEDNESDAY	THURSDAY	FRIDAY
SUBJECT	Time:					
TEACHER	Room:					
SUBJECT	Time:					
TEACHER	Room:					
SUBJECT	Time:					
TEACHER	Room:					
SUBJECT	Time:					
TEACHER	Room:					
SUBJECT	Time:					
TEACHER	Room:					
SUBJECT	Time:					
TEACHER	Room:					

DIRECTIONS: FIRST, ask your teachers the exact days, times, and places when they are available to help students. **THEN,** circle the times that best match your "free" time.

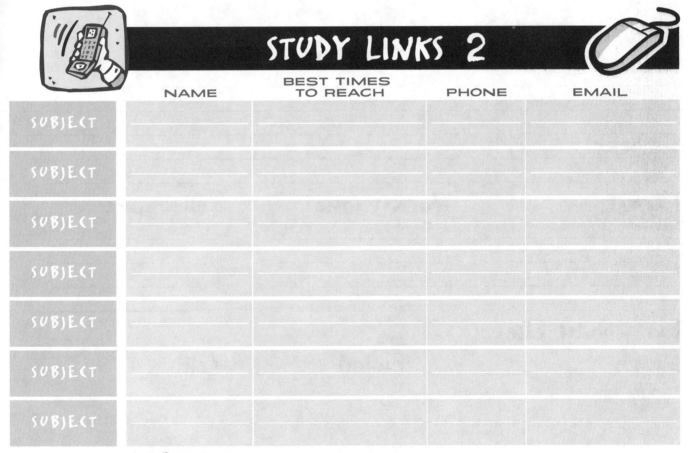

STUDY LINKS 2

	NAME	BEST TIMES TO REACH	PHONE	EMAIL
SUBJECT				
SUBJECT				
SUBJECT				
SUBJECT				
SUBJECT				
SUBJECT				
SUBJECT				

DIRECTIONS: In each subject, find two classmates you can depend on for help if you get stuck. Then fill in the information above.

PERSONAL DIRECTORY

School Main Number_____

Teachers' Voice Mail Numbers

Name: Name:

_____   _____
_____   _____
_____   _____
_____

Homework Hotline:_____
Coach's Name & Tel. No.:_____ - ____
Coach's Name & Tel. No.:_____ - ____
Local Library:_____ Library Hours:_____

Favorite Search Engines:
Web Addresses

_____   _____
_____   _____
_____   _____
_____   _____
_____   _____

Parent   Work phone   Cell phone

_____   _____   _____
_____   _____   _____
_____   _____   _____

Everybody Else:

Name   Email   Cell   Tel.

_____   _____
_____   _____
_____   _____
_____   _____
_____   _____

ABBREVIATIONS & NOTATIONS

Use these abbreviations and notations to write faster when notetaking and to save space in your Homework Organizer.

Verbs/Action Words

ans	answer
ck	check
corr	correct
def	define
est	estimate
expl.	explain
fd	find
hdout	handout
lk up	look up
lrn	learn
mem	memorize
outl	outline
prev	preview
rd	read
resched	reschedule
rev	review
rewr	rewrite
rm	room
sched	schedule
sum	summarize
trans	translate
wrt	write

NOUNS

ass't	assignment
avg	average
bk	book
ch.	chapter
defn	definition
dict'y	dictionary

dir.	directions
dit	ditto
ency	encyclopedia
est	estimate
ex.	example
exper.	experiment
fig.	figure
gr.	grade
gram	grammar
intro	introduction
par	paragraph
pg.	page
Q	question
rdg	reading
rept	report
schl	school
spellg	spelling
syn	synonym
tchr	teacher
voc	vocabulary
vol.	volume
wkbk	workbook
wrtg	writing

NOTATIONS

Ø	none (no homework)
¶	paragraph
#	number
*	important!
+	and
>	more, larger than, after
<	less, smaller than, before

@	at
ea.	each
-g =	l-ingl as in "spellg"
-mt =	l-mentl as in "agreemt"
-tn =	l-tionl as in "reactn"
w/	with
w/o	without

LATIN

c. or ca.	about
cf.	compare
etc.	and so forth
et al.	and others
e.g.	for example
i.e.	that is
n.b.	note well
[sic]	written exactly as in the original
viz.	namely
vs.	versus
v.v	vice versa

MINE

INDEX OF EVERYTHING IN THIS BOOK